# YOU CAN BE A
# MOVIE
# EXTRA

## The Complete Guide to Working as a Supporting Artiste in Film and TV

G000082325

# ROB
# MARTIN

## TITAN BOOKS

**YOU CAN BE A MOVIE EXTRA**
1 84023 522 5

Published by
Titan Books
A division of
Titan Publishing Group Ltd
144 Southwark St
London
SE1 0UP

First edition September 2002
10 9 8 7 6 5 4 3 2 1

**Acknowledgements**
This book is for my girlfriend Tracey, who showed remarkable patience and understanding while it was being written, late at night after my day job. I would also like to thank all my friends and family for their encouragement, particularly Mum and Dad. Thanks to all at Titan Books, especially Adam Newell. Thanks also to all the production crews who have shown their support for The Casting Collective, all the SAs who generously took the time to contribute (sorry there wasn't room to fit you all in) and to those who understand how difficult the casting agent's job can be. Finally, thanks to the best casting team in the world: Laura, Sarah, Rosie, Chloe, Lloyd and Simon. — **Rob Martin**

The publishers would also like to thank Josef Accerelli, Daniel Baggs, Stephanie Barrows, Jos Dewing, Ray Donn, Lindsay Elliott, Ken Farmer, Nick Field, Graham Frosdick, Colin Giffin, Jeremy C. A. Goad, Sue Hallet, Ron Harrison, Philip Harvey, Mike Jones, Malcolm Lauder, James Lowe, Richard Manlove, Ambrose Pigott, John Random, Albert Ratcliffe, Bella Sabbagh, Nobuko Slater, Laura Tilly, Lucy Wallis and Kerry-ann Willing for their contributions to this book.

**Publisher's Note**
Every effort has been made to ensure that the information given in this book was correct at the time of going to press, and the advice included herein is given in good faith. However, details and circumstances change. This book is intended as a guide only: the publishers cannot accept responsibility for any consequences arising from its use.

# CONTENTS

# INTRODUCTION

## FIRST THINGS FIRST — WHY AN EXTRA ISN'T REALLY AN EXTRA

Background Artiste. Walk-on. Non-speaking or simply Crowd — there are many different terms to describe Extras, and they're all commonly heard on set. For the purposes of this book though, the term Supporting Artiste, or SA, will cover all of these.

Those already working in the industry frown on the term 'Extra', as it has connotations of being 'extra to requirements'. This certainly isn't the case. Just imagine the *Gladiator* arena without the roar of the spectators, or the opening battle scene of *Saving Private Ryan* without the soldiers. Or how about the theatre in *Shakespeare in Love* with no audience? Supporting Artistes are a very important element of the film-making process. And it's not just in the movies that SAs have a part to play. While this book focuses mainly on what most people will be interested in — feature films and television — as a successful SA you are also likely to work on commercials, pop videos, photographic stills, corporate training videos and the Internet, so the book will cover those kinds of jobs too.

## THE THREE MAIN AIMS OF THIS BOOK

Firstly, this book will help newcomers to the business assess how suitable they are for work as a Supporting Artiste, breaking down the many myths that surround the job. For example, it seems that everyone knows someone, who knows someone, who worked on a film or a TV soap and earned a lot of money for 'standing around all day not doing anything'. The job of an SA is not as simple as that, of course. An Assistant Director recently told me that when she first started her job and found out how much SAs were paid, she thought it was way too much. But she went on to say that three or four years down the line, she now thinks that they actually deserve every penny they get, if not more!

Secondly, this book will adopt a step-by-step approach for those who think they are suitable and want to go beyond the stage of just talking about being an SA, enabling you to actually have a go. Whilst it has been known for some lucky people who look right for a particular role to be plucked off the street, this is not the norm. This book goes beyond luck. It will arm you with the inside knowledge you need to make yourself more appealing to the agencies that cast SAs (and I should know, as I'm an SA agent myself). How do you find a good agent? How do agents work? How do you get your first job? Do you need to join a union? What should you expect to find in a contract? What happens on the filming day? How do you get paid? These are just a few of the questions that will be answered.

The final aim is to help those already working as SAs to fulfil their potential, and get the maximum amount of work possible. Whilst researching this book, I've come across a lot of advice suggesting that 'anyone can be an Extra', or that you 'do not need any special skills to be an Extra'. As will become clear, neither of those statements is necessarily true. To be successful, by which I mean to regularly be offered work, is not so easy. This book is an essential guide to help you achieve just that. It will also discuss what you can aim for beyond being a face in the crowd. How can you progress from being in the background to being a featured Walk-on, and ultimately an actor?

## 'HOLLYWOOD' IN BRITAIN

The British film industry conforms to many British stereotypes. It is fairly unassuming and modest, yet incredibly good at what it does. The industry goes way beyond typically 'British' films like *Notting Hill*, *Trainspotting* or *Billy Elliot*. I have been involved in casting SAs for a lot of big-budget 'Hollywood' films that were actually made in the UK — *Gladiator*, *The Mummy*, *Tomb Raider*, *Spy Game*, *Sleepy Hollow* and *Eyes Wide Shut*, to give you a few examples. There are plenty more: England has always been the home of the James Bond series, the first four *Star Wars* films were made here and, more recently, there's been *Harry Potter and the Philosopher's Stone*, the first of up to seven Potter movies which will presumably all be filmed in the UK.

It is often said that the UK has the finest film technicians in the world.

Supporting Artistes in the UK have an equally fine reputation, and if you are going to be successful as one, you really need to know what you are doing. It is a very competitive world out there! Although its primary aim is to explore working as an SA in the UK, both in and around London and the various regional centres, we will also look briefly at how the industry operates globally — how things differ in the USA, and around the world.

You don't have to take just my word for all this. Throughout the book, you'll find helpful advice and some entertaining stories, kindly supplied by people currently working in the business as Supporting Artistes.

This book won't make you rich. It won't make you into an actor (if you don't have an ounce of talent), and it won't guarantee you invitations to any premières. But I hope that *You Can Be a Movie Extra* succeeds in its aim to be, in essence, the Bible for both the new and the experienced Supporting Artiste.

# GETTING STARTED

In relation to the stars, the Director, or the Producer, Supporting Artistes are usually seen as being pretty low down in the pecking order of a production. After all, there is no Oscar for Best Film Extra (not yet, anyway). However, SAs can often be essential to a production's success. When you watch a film or TV drama you naturally follow the action between the central characters. But to create atmosphere on screen, there are always lots of other things going on in the background that make you believe in what you are looking at. Just as important as the costumes, the special effects, the location or the props are the Supporting Artistes. But as we will discover, there can be a lot more to working as an SA than just being moving scenery.

It's intriguing to see how fascinating most people find the idea of being a Supporting Artiste. Anyone could be one, it seems. They offer the audience a sense of realism. Take the Queen Vic pub in *EastEnders*: equally as important as the pub set itself is the people in it — one wouldn't work without the other. There are all kinds of dramas, involving every walk of life. In appearance at least, being an SA is truly an equal opportunities profession.

## DEFINITIONS

So what exactly is a Supporting Artiste? Moreover, how do you know the difference between an SA, a Walk-on and an actor? Just to be clear, here are some definitions provided by Equity, the actors' union. A Supporting Artiste is someone "who appears in vision (other than members of the public in actuality scenes) who shall not be required to give individual characterisation or speak any dialogue". In less confusing words, someone in a crowd of people, or someone in the background of the scene.

The middle ground between an SA and an actor is called a Walk-on. A Walk-on is someone "who is required to exercise their professional skills in relation to a cast actor and/or in close up to camera and be required to impersonate an identifiable individual and/or speak a few unimportant words which shall not have an effect on the overall script or outcome of the story". In other words, someone the viewer is more likely to identify as an individual.

At the top of the tree, above SAs and Walk-ons, are the actors. 'Actor' covers everything from the principal characters down to small roles. The distinction between a Walk-on and an actor in a very small part is sometimes fairly murky, but as a general rule an actor is more likely to deliver dialogue. This doesn't mean that if you are not a trained actor you will never be asked to do any dialogue. It's just that, as we will go on to explore, any production casts its actors and its Supporting Artistes completely separately right from the beginning.

## SO HOW DOES IT WORK?

On any production, the person ultimately responsible for the SAs is the Producer. Whilst you are actually on set, you become the responsibility of the Assistant Director (1st AD). They usually delegate responsibility to the Second Assistant Director (2nd AD). On bigger productions a Crowd Assistant Director will be appointed to deal solely with organising the SAs and perhaps some of the smaller parts. But where have these SAs come from? That's where an Extras casting agency comes in. The Assistant Director will appoint an agency to actually cast and supply all of the Supporting Artistes. (The exception to this may be if a production is filming in an area where there are no agencies. The Crowd AD's job will then be to cast the SAs himself from local people, or organise SAs to be brought in from another area.)

## THE DIVIDE BETWEEN ACTORS AND SUPPORTING ARTISTES

The production normally hands responsibility for finding the actors to a Casting Director. It's rare for the paths of the Casting Director finding the actors, and the Extras agency searching for the SAs, to actually cross. The two normally have separate budgets and, let's face it, separate skills and agendas. (The exception to this may be the Walk-on parts, which may be cast by either, or both.)

A Casting Director's main aim is to work with the Director to get the best possible performer to fit the role in question. They will spend a long time organising script readings with dozens of different actors to find the right performer. They may also work on behalf of the Producer in negotiating a principal actor's fee with his or her agent.

I should point out that actors' agents and Supporting Artistes' agents are very different. An actors' agent will have a much smaller number of people on their books, and their role is to put their clients up for the right parts. Supporting Artistes' agents can have thousands of people on their books. Although performance skills can be important for Supporting Artistes, the agency casting the background is much more concerned with the overall look of the crowd. The SA agent's role is also more logistical in terms of organising and supplying sometimes hundreds of people for a production, as opposed to a few cast parts.

As a general rule, actors' agents do not like their artistes to do background work; they think it will undermine their status as an actor. For this reason Casting Directors tend to look down a bit on Supporting Artistes, and it is extremely unlikely that a Casting Director will consider you for a role in a production unless you have an acting agent. You are more likely to get your 'big break' beyond background work in spontaneous moments on set, when a Director will pull someone forward from the crowd to do a line of dialogue or act out a reaction to camera. (Believe me, this can and does happen, as a few of the stories from SAs in Chapter 7 show.)

While it is possible to be a Supporting Artiste just by being in the right place at the right time (sometimes productions use 'street castings', literally pulling people in off the street for a job), the majority of work is given to SAs registered with agencies. The next chapter explains how to get an agent, but at this stage it would be useful to dispel the myth that anyone can work on a regular basis. There are a number of factors that restrict your suitability for background work. Before you take the plunge, read the following to assess your likelihood of making it onto the screen.

## FACTORS YOU CAN'T INFLUENCE — 'ORDINARY' OR 'EXTRAORDINARY'?

The secret to regular work is not so much skill, but versatility. Unfortunately, the major part of this has already been decided for you — because your versatility is mainly dependent on what you look like. Those who work as Supporting Artistes fall into two types of physical appearance. These types can be defined by two words: 'ordinary' and 'extraordinary'.

## The 'Ordinary' Type

The 'ordinary' type is someone of average height. For men that means 5 feet 7 inches to 6 feet 2 inches, and for women 5 feet 4 inches to 5 feet 10 inches. Their facial features are non-specific; they do not have sticking-out ears for example, or a big nose. Their body type is average; not particularly over or under weight. They are not covered in piercings or tattoos. In essence, they are people who do not stand out from the crowd. Their age, sex and skin type are not as important, because all types are used.

However, it should be noted that individuals do need to fit the time period and location in which the production is set. For example, most of the exterior filming for *The Mummy* and *The Mummy Returns* was shot in Morocco (and set in Egypt), so when the productions came to the UK for studio work, I had the job of matching those types of people for the interior shots. The SAs we cast were therefore mainly of Middle Eastern or North African appearance. On the Robert Redford/Brad Pitt thriller *Spy Game* the stakes were raised even higher — we needed to find 200 Chinese people for a scene set in a Chinese prison that was actually shot in Oxford. Similarly, for the Arctic sequences in *Tomb Raider* we had to find Inuits for the interior studio work.

Casting for the period military drama *The Four Feathers*, we had a greater demand for men, most of whom were white, since the majority were playing 1880s soldiers. As well as your sex, age can also be restrictive; obviously no pensioners were cast as the young soldiers in *The Four Feathers*. However, there is no upper age limit to working as a Supporting Artiste. There are some in their eighties who still work regularly; the oldest person on our books is eighty-seven. So long as you have your health, retirement as a Supporting Artiste is not an issue.

## The 'Extraordinary' Type

The 'extraordinary' type is someone who is picked because they have a certain look — they *do* stand out from the crowd. These SAs could be picked out individually to appear in what's known as a 'feature' (ie, they will be specifically featured onscreen during a scene), or they may be selected to give a realistic representation of a group. For example, any present-day big city street scene will need to reflect an accurate slice of society. This may include, in a crowd of 100, two or three very tall people, some overweight people, some men with long hair and perhaps someone in a wheelchair.

In a smaller crowd, the distribution of representative types may be different. Imagine a scene set in a small town in Cornwall, with the camera close up on two principal actors. In the background are two passers-by. A punky-looking woman with a shaved head walks past with her boyfriend, who has a big Afro haircut. Unless this couple is important to the development of the story they would probably stand out too much in this scene, distracting from the main action. On the other hand, when a production actually needs a woman with a shaved head and a man with an Afro, only these types will do. Occasionally the casting agency may receive a brief that calls for interesting or 'character-full' faces. Some Directors, especially on films like *Harry Potter* or *Sleepy Hollow*, may be looking to set a tone or feeling with the types of people in the background.

There is an interesting paradox between the two groups. The 'ordinary' people will tend to get more work offered to them simply because they fit into more scenes, and they can therefore earn more money. However, while the 'extraordinary' type may be offered less work, the work they do get may be considerably better paid.

As you consider becoming a Supporting Artiste, ask yourself which type you are: 'ordinary' or 'extraordinary'. This will be your first guide to your suitability and, ultimately, how often you will be used as an SA.

## WORK FOR THE UNDER-SIXTEENS

As I've pointed out, there's no upper age limit to getting work as an SA. But there are quite a few factors to take into account regarding children, and it's worth going into a bit of detail about them here.

In 1998 the law in the UK became considerably stricter about those under sixteen working on any set. It is possible, but requires a licence from the local authority (LEA) where the child lives. This may take up to twenty-one days to organise. The application must be accompanied by the child's birth certificate and two identical photographs (one of which is retained by the LEA), taken no more than six months before the application. The LEA may make any enquiries necessary to satisfy itself that it should grant a licence. For example: it may request a report from the child's head teacher. It may request that the child be medically examined in order to establish their fitness, and that the child's health will not suffer by taking part in the performances. It can even interview the applicant, the parents and the proposed chaperone and private/on-set teacher (the child's education must continue if filming takes place during term time).

Under-sixteens need to have a registered chaperone to look after them on set (which is another cost to the production). Children also have restrictions on the number of hours they are allowed to work during any one day. These are broken down into three age ranges — nine to fifteen years, five to eight years and under five years — with the youngest having the most restrictive hours. The nature of film work is such that schedules change; it is quite normal for a filming day to be rescheduled two or three times before it happens, and this can cause further paperwork. Because of these restrictions a production may use young adults if it can get away with it; it is quite normal for a production looking for people to play thirteen to fifteen year-old characters to use young-looking sixteen and seventeen year-olds.

The licence also prevents children working for more than a set number of days in any year, in order to stop children missing too much school. The *Harry Potter* films being shot in the UK at the moment tend to cast child actors and SAs from stage schools that have the paperwork ready to licence each child as and when they are needed. There is nothing to prevent a production getting a licence for child SAs itself, and occasionally it does happen. For example, a production may need to film at a school, and will get permission from the LEA to use everyone in the school it selects as a location. Nevertheless, on the whole it is pretty difficult to work regularly as a Supporting Artiste if you're under the age of sixteen.

The pay for background children is also fairly poor, as they normally only receive half the adult rate. The exception to this may be children who do featured work, and for that you would need to join a specialist child agency. These agencies look for children who have the commitment and talent to do featured acting work as well as background work. A list of these child agencies can be found at the back of this book.

## FACTORS YOU CAN INFLUENCE

Don't despair: there are factors you *can* influence when it comes to getting work as a Supporting Artiste, though be aware that they do tend to require quite a bit of commitment.

## Your Ability to Perform

All Directors would agree that at least a degree of natural talent is vital when it comes to performing in front of the camera. In terms of working as an SA however, your acting ability is not necessarily as important as your appearance. Nevertheless, even in the background there are some general rules to follow. The most important thing is not to *over*act. It's worth remembering that when you are on screen, the slightest action can appear exaggerated. If you are required to take any direction, remember that the camera comes to you, rather than you trying to grab the camera's attention. Unlike the theatre where all actions need to be overstated to reach the audience, the camera is much more subtle. That is why working in local theatre may not necessarily give you the best start in terms of how to behave in front of camera. There is nothing worse for a Director than to ask someone to do a simple action and for that person to exaggerate the performance so much that it becomes unnatural and, at best, fairly comical. As long as you are confident, acting experience is not essential to start out as an SA. It may help you in terms of basic confidence if you have successfully worked in local theatre or amateur productions, but the two styles are very different.

## Hair Length

Getting hair length right is always a struggle for Supporting Artistes. It is completely dependent on what is currently in production. A TV drama set in medieval England may require men to grow their hair longer over the collar. Yet on another production set in Edwardian England, they may be required to have long hair on top, but very short back and sides. Both could be filming at the same time. It can sometimes be difficult to judge which way to go! This problem is not exclusive to men. Women with modern haircuts can ruin their chances of working on a period drama. SAs often question why they cannot be wigged for a production. Years ago productions may have considered wigging Supporting Artistes. Today however, budget restrictions dictate that if you look right but have the wrong hair, the agent will be asked to find someone who looks right *and* has the right hair. Period drama will not allow for men or women with highlights or dyed hair, or any style that looks too modern. (It's also worth mentioning here that suntans are usually not allowed in period productions either.)

Quite often, SAs get a long run on a production because of their hair. The production then finishes and the work seems to stop. They then wonder about getting their hair cut or growing it long. This is a personal decision, of course, but one thing I would say is this: if you're a man who normally has long hair, or a woman with very short hair, it may be worth leaving it that way. There are, after all, a lot fewer men with long hair and women with short hair than the other way around these days, so your chances of being used as an 'extraordinary' type are greater.

## Where You Live

Another important factor is your location in relation to the production's location. All productions have a very tight budget. In ninety-nine per cent of cases there is little or no budget for travel or accommodation for Supporting Artistes. Sometimes those SAs that do well may happen to live near a studio, but this is not essential. You can live anywhere if you have the commitment to travel. Some SAs regularly travel to London from the Midlands or live in London and will travel to Bristol for work.

I have to stress that if you don't have a car, you are heavily restricting yourself. Often locations will be away from main forms of public transport. Some SAs do perfectly well without driving, but they tend to be based in major filming cities such as London or Manchester where public transport is good. Because filming hours are particularly long and often involve very early starts, if you need to travel for more than an hour and a half to get to filming locations you may need to think twice about committing to working as an SA. If you don't drive it's not the end of the world, it just means you need to be a lot more organised — get all available bus and train timetables, taxi numbers and a mobile phone. The latter is something *every* SA needs. Trying to do this job without a mobile is not advisable!

It's worth noting that if you are from outside the EU you will normally require a work permit to work in the UK. Most productions receive tax incentives to employ people that are part of the EU.

## Availability

To the agent, this is the single most important aspect of any Supporting Artiste. You can be an incredibly versatile-looking person who seems to fit every casting brief and is always in demand, but if you're not available you're as good as useless. A small number of people work as Supporting Artistes as their only source of income. Known in the industry as the 'professionals' they have no problem with availability. These people — perhaps numbering less than 1,000 in the UK — have usually spent a long time working before they were comfortable enough to rely solely on their SA income. If you are just starting out, stick to the old cliché: 'Don't give up the day job!'

If you have a full-time job and you are not the boss, or cannot take multiple days off at very short notice, you will not be suitable for work as a Supporting Artiste. An exception to this may be if a big production happens to be filming close by to you. Often that production will be keen to use some local people and you may decide to take some of your holiday to work on it.

One of my biggest jobs was casting the opening battle scene in *Gladiator*. This was filmed at Bourne Wood just outside Farnham in Surrey. Being fifty miles from London, and with very early starts to the filming, the production wanted to use local people, avoiding the hassle of bringing in crowds of up to 800 people a day from outside the area. We organised a casting at the local arts centre and soon had a pool of 2,000 local people all keen to go into battle, with only the front line being experienced SAs that were brought in from London. However, the nature of filming is such that schedules change, and often dates that individuals had been given as their filming days moved, sometimes at short notice. Some local people were caught out, taking a week off and then finding that the days they had been pencilled in for had changed to the following week. During the filming of this sequence, the people who did well were those who were self-employed and therefore flexible with their work schedule, and those with part-time jobs, who simply had more time to spare. (Plus there were the retired, some students and a few rich eccentrics!)

The amount of notice you will be given for potential work is typically a few days if you're lucky. Often you will be called at very short notice, perhaps the afternoon before a shoot. Occasionally, if someone has dropped out, you may be asked if you can work today! Therefore if you are flexible enough to drop everything, you are likely to be used more often. If you do have a part-time job, be aware that you will need to be available for whole days. Being available Tuesday and Wednesdays after 2pm is not helpful. A filming day will nearly always mean the *whole* day. You will not be looked upon favourably if you suddenly announce to the set that you have to leave at 5pm to go to your other job.

If you are only available evenings and weekends, it's not really worth planning a new secondary income. Filming is a seven-days-a-week, 365-

days-a-year process, and while it is true that filming does take place at weekends and at night, continuity dictates that you will be needed throughout the week as well. It is therefore unlikely that any agent will take people on who are only available weekends and evenings. However, an exception can be made if you have an in-demand special skill, or belong to an ethnic group that's in short supply when it comes to SAs. Here's a story from an SA who fell into the latter category:

I have a full-time job in finance in London. In the past year, though, I have seen myself in the films *Tomb Raider*, *Spy Game* and *Legally Blonde*. It all began when I fancied doing something completely different from my day job, just for fun. I fancied becoming a Supporting Artiste... meeting the movie stars...

So one day during my lunch hour at work, I started searching the Internet for casting agencies. I stumbled on one that advertised for immediate castings on its website. It was looking for 'businessmen wearing smart clothes', for *Tomb Raider*. Being immersed in a business environment practically all year round, I thought I might have a chance. I quickly fired off an email, giving a brief description of myself. I went back to doing my day job when, that very afternoon, I had a reply from the agency. It was completely unexpected — after all, I had thought it was very difficult to get work in this line of business. They wanted some photographs, so I sent them a close-up portrait shot and another one of me standing wearing a business suit.

They must have liked the photos, because a month later, I was on location filming a scene for *Tomb Raider*. The agency invited me to register on their casting book later that year, even though I could only do it at weekends. I only work about ten days a year as a Supporting Artiste, and that suits me fine. I'm already looking forward to spotting myself in the second *Harry Potter* film. I can only say that I was at the right website at the right time!

**Nobuko Slater**

## DO YOU HAVE THE RIGHT TYPE OF PERSONALITY?

Ask yourself these questions: Can you get up at 4am, after only managing to get to bed at midnight the night before? Can you stand in line, waiting to get home, without getting grumpy? Can you keep your spirits up when it's wet and cold? If these questions don't make you break out in a sweat, you may be the right kind of person to do background work.

Working as an SA you could experience some of the most memorable moments of your life. But if your personality is not suited, you could experience some of the most miserable. I've known people beg to leave a set because it hasn't lived up to what they've expected. On any set you are going to meet some really interesting people, and some that are maybe, well, not so interesting. If you're the sort of person who needs their own private space, or you don't enjoy being stuck with the same group of people for long periods of time, this job is not for you.

The the greatest 'skill' you can have as a Supporting Artiste is patience. Sometimes hours can pass with nothing happening. It may be cold, it may be too hot. Your Elizabethan costume may look great on, but itches like hell. The SAs who are appreciated the most by the crew are the ones that don't complain unnecessarily. Sometimes you may be completely within your rights to complain, but there is a right way and a wrong way of doing this. It is always important to remember that you may be on the set for one or two days, while crew members can be there every day, six or seven days a week for months with little time to rest. For this reason, fuses can sometimes be a little shorter than is normal in daily life, and the SAs that rub people up the wrong way are the ones that won't be asked to come back. If you do have a complaint, talk to your agent first — that's what they are there for. It is also equally important to be nice to your agent! Also bear in mind that it's worth being polite to your fellow artistes. After all you may get stuck, and need a lift home...

Finally, working as an SA does not make you a star. Prima donna types need not apply. If you have the sort of personality that demands individual attention, or will have a strop about wearing that particular shade of green, working in the background is probably a bad idea. Crew members have their work cut out dealing with the real stars, and they will not tolerate this kind of behaviour from the Supporting Artistes.

## DO YOU NEED TO JOIN A UNION?

To most people, joining a union is not the most interesting aspect of the job. Nevertheless it's worth knowing a little about how unions work, and how you can make them work for you. In the UK there are two unions that look after the interests of Supporting Artistes: the FAA (Film Artistes' Association, part of BECTU, the Broadcasting Entertainment Cinematographic and Theatre Union) and Equity. Working as an SA used to be a fairly closed shop, and it was rare for non-union members to be offered work. Nowadays you do not have to belong to any union to work as a Supporting Artiste. However, there certainly are advantages. Unions are important because they protect your pay and your rights when you work on any production. It is their job to negotiate agreements setting out the terms and conditions of your employment, so joining one will help protect you and your earnings. Without them, artistes would be pushed into working longer and longer hours for less and less money.

To the newcomer, it's rather confusing having two unions that appear, on the surface, to do a similar job. A bit of history may help clarify this. The FAA was originally formed in 1927, but by the early 90s was finding it increasingly difficult to support itself, and needed to amalgamate with a bigger organisation to survive. Initially it tried to transfer to Equity, the actors' union. However, Equity members are not just those working in film and TV, they cover a broad spectrum of the Arts and Entertainment industry, and have been accused in the past of being fairly snobby towards Supporting Artistes. Equity declined the offer. Wanting to stay in a related organisation, the FAA became part of BECTU.

Currently Equity and the FAA both look after the interests of SAs, but the FAA's remit is far narrower than Equity's, both in terms of types of jobs, and geographically. The FAA is only really effective with feature films and independent television productions in and around London. They have an agreement with PACT (Producers' Alliance for Cinema and Television) that SAs should be paid a certain rate when working on productions filming within a forty-mile radius of Charing Cross in central London. With the exception of BBC-Equity/PACT productions and ITV-Equity/PACT productions, the Equity agreement does not cover Supporting Artistes within this area.

Outside of the forty miles, Equity does have an agreement with PACT that set rates are paid to SAs. However, this agreement is not as effective as the FAA agreement, as rates can be negotiated if the production is employing more than forty-one SAs in any one day (and can therefore end up lower than the normal set rate). Equity also has a separate agreement with TAC (Welsh Independent Producers) for those working on Welsh productions, and advises on pay for other types of work, such as commercials. (See Chapter 6 for more details on rates of pay and union agreements.)

To join Equity you need to show evidence of six days' work undertaken on Equity contracts over a period of twelve consecutive months. Unfortunately they do not recognise any work undertaken under the FAA agreement as a means of joining Equity. Equity currently has an entrance fee of £25 and an annual subscription of £60. The FAA currently has an annual fee of £60.

If you only work occasionally, joining a union may not seem crucial or cost effective. Nevertheless, if you start to get offered work regularly, joining Equity or the FAA, or both, is very sensible. The more members they have, the easier the unions will find it to protect your proper rates of pay from Producers always looking to cut costs. Belonging to a union will also benefit you if something goes wrong on set or with your payments.

Contact details for the FAA and Equity can be found at the back of the book.

## CAN YOU PASS THE TEST?

Spend a minute doing this simple test. If you can say yes to the following questions you have a good chance of being able to get regular work as a Supporting Artiste.

**1** Do you look fairly average in height, size and physical features? ❑

**2** Are you over sixteen years of age? ❑

**3** Have you had experience performing in front of people? ❑

**4** Are you a confident person? ❑

**5** Do you live in a location that has filming regularly taking place near by? ❑

**6** Are you available to work during the week as well as week-ends? ❏

**7** Are you available to work at short notice? ❏

**8** Are you available to work complete days rather than just parts of days? ❏

**9** Are you a citizen of a country in the European Union? ❏

**10** Do you have a friendly, cooperative personality? ❏

**11** Are you patient, with a good sense of humour? ❏

**12** Do you drive or are you good with public transport? ❏

**13** Do you have a mobile phone? ❏

**14** Are you good at getting up in the morning? ❏

**15** Are you OK about being told what to do? ❏

**16** Do you accept that this type of work has little glamour and will not make you famous? ❏

# FINDING AN AGENT

If you're exceptionally lucky, and know the right people, you can get work on a production as a Supporting Artiste without an agent. People hired 'direct' are usually friends of the crew, or friends of friends. You might have seen a couple of recent, high profile examples of this: Steven Spielberg turned up in a party scene in *Vanilla Sky* (starring his friend Tom Cruise), and Mick Jagger and his daughter can be spotted as Extras in *Enigma* (a film Jagger just happened to produce). If you are found in a street casting you may be lucky, but nine times out of ten, you will only be offered work by an agency you have registered with.

Bear in mind this is not *Jerry Maguire*. You will not have a personal agent who comes round to your house, so you can shout "Show me the Money!" at him. You will be one among hundreds. It is of course your agent's responsibility to find you work, but it doesn't stop there. They are responsible for the way you are treated on set, but also for the way *you* behave (if an SA causes trouble, it's the agency that takes the blame). The agent also makes sure you get paid correctly and on time, and deals with any disputes that arise concerning your pay and your general welfare (though some agencies are more responsible about this than others). It's fair to say that choosing the right agency (or agencies) will directly affect how much work you are offered.

## SOME HISTORY

Up until the 1980s, working as an SA was a fairly closed shop. You had to be an Equity or FAA member to work on a TV programme or film. There was one predominant organisation called Central Casting that for many years controlled the majority of work for SAs. Then the inevitable happened. Several rival companies were started by agents who'd previously worked for Central Casting, and, along with the influence of various political events, the closed shop was busted open. History has repeated itself several times over the last twenty years, with staff from the older agencies leaving to set up new ones of their own. Some quickly disappear and some do well — the film industry is like a roller-coaster ride, it's all about highs and lows. The middle ground never really seems to happen, it is either extremely busy or completely quiet. At times of growth, when the industry is busy, the cycle begins again and more new agencies start to appear.

Today in the UK there are over fifty agencies that claim to offer work for Supporting Artistes. However, there are probably less than ten that do ninety-nine per cent of all the work. In and around the London area, where there are perhaps twenty agencies in total, only three or four are worth considering joining. It's therefore really important that you find the right one for you. Since the government and the unions have fought hard to outlaw the rogue agents, the next five years is a time when only the strongest, busiest agencies will survive.

## CHOOSING YOUR AGENT

The golden rule is: do your research. Ask around and find out which agencies have good reputations and which do not. If you know people who already work in the industry, quiz them for advice. Do not assume that all agencies are reputable. Have a look at the list of established agencies at the back of the book — this will be a good starting point, but bear in mind that this is a fast-changing industry, so it is worth doing your own research. If you want more names and phone numbers, get hold of a copy of an industry manual, such as *The Knowledge* published by United Business Media, or *Kays* published by Kay Media Ltd. These manuals are designed for production crew members and are expensive to buy, but you should be able to find them in any good library. A cheaper alternative is *Contacts* published by The Spotlight (normally £9.99). All of these will give you a list of agencies with contact details, but remember the company has paid to advertise, so it doesn't necessarily follow that because they have an advert they are a good agency. It's also worth remembering that a good agency to one person may be a bad agency to another, so try to get a broad consensus, rather than just one person's opinion.

If you don't know anyone already working as an SA, have a look on the Internet. There are a few websites where SAs swap advice; a couple are listed at the back of this book. Agency websites are also listed at the back — you can visit them to get a feel for the size of the company, and how busy they are, as most have a list of credits of the productions they have worked on. However, be aware that these lists may not always be entirely accurate. Certain agencies exaggerate their success, implying that they have supplied all the SAs for a project, when in fact they have only supplied one specific artiste to a production. In fact, one agency was taken to court for doing this.

Once you have decided on a shortlist of agencies, the next step is to ring them and ask when they are registering new clients. Remember, agencies are very busy places, so try not to ring at the wrong times. Bad times are usually in the late afternoon or evening, when they are preparing for who is on set the following day. Do not ring them at weekends or turn up at their office unannounced. It may seem like a good idea, but you'll only end up making a nuisance of yourself. Agencies are dealing with hundreds of people at any given time and when they are not looking for new people, they only take initial enquiries by phone, post or email, not in person.

Some agencies specialise in particular types of people; there are agencies that only take on ethnic minorities, tall people, short people, bald people or even ugly people. Some agencies specialise in specific types of work — some do more pop videos, or commercials, or feature films — whilst some cover all areas. If you're only interested in being in movies, don't join an agency that rarely works on them. Also find out what level of work the agency can offer you. If you are more experienced and hoping for more featured and Walk-on roles, don't join an agency that only does background work.

The biggest problem with finding an agency is that the ones worth joining tend to be the ones that are hardest to join. However, good timing can increase your chances considerably. Most agencies do put aside time to register new people at some point, normally annually, although some only do it every two years. By ringing the agency, finding out when they are registering, and then applying at the time when they are actively looking for fresh faces, you stand a much better chance of getting onto their books.

## DODGY AGENTS

Be careful — some companies out there have no intention of finding you any work. Thanks to the Department of Trade and Industry it has become harder for scam agencies to exist, but some still do. Here's a real horror story from an SA who got caught up in a scam, followed by a checklist which will help make sure the same thing doesn't happen to you:

Like many Supporting Artistes who believe they are capable of bettering themselves in the industry, now and again I try new agencies that might give me better prospects. Answering an ad I'd seen in a London evening paper, I was asked to the agency's office for a meeting, and was introduced to a fat geezer with a cockney accent and a big cigar. He started to tell me how 'this could be me' — pointing to a picture of Steve McFadden and other *EastEnders* stars. I gave him my details, and work receipts (which he kept) of previous work from other agencies. By the second meeting, I had agreed to pay him a joining fee, and wrote a cheque for £130, made payable to (believe it or not) a Mr A. Daley. But this didn't seem like an Arthur Daley outfit! The location of the offices, and the hordes of other Extras made it seem above board. The third week I had a photo shoot, supposedly for the agency's book.

The following week he promised to take me for an Italian meal in a restaurant down below the offices — but this was postponed. We arranged to meet the following Friday instead. However England was playing Argentina and again our meeting was postponed. I heard nothing about any work. By this point, I was beginning to worry that this was a bogus operation. I was proved right: he became totally uncontactable. I tried phoning several times, without success. I tried to visit him at his offices, and after several attempts when the receptionist kept telling me he was out, I tried to make my way upstairs regardless, but was turned away, and then stopped from entering the building by the security guards.

Two years down the line, and several county court cases later, I was informed that the person who had taken my cheque had actually passed away! Obviously I felt angry and frustrated with this whole experience — and I never got my £130 back.

**Josef Accerelli**

## SCAMS

Here are four danger signs to watch out for:

1 Do not join an agency that doesn't require meeting you in person. If they haven't met you, how do they know if you are suitable for work?

2 Do not join an agency that only has a PO Box address. This may suggest they haven't actually got an office.

3 The FAA advises that you should never pay an agent any registration fee up front. In recent years a lot of con artists have set up agencies that demand a registration fee of anything between £30 and £250 up front. They then disappear as quickly as they appeared — with your money.

4 Avoid agencies that advertise for new people regularly. Unless they are looking for a particular type of person they are short of, legitimate agencies don't really need to advertise for new applicants.

While not actually 'scam' outfits, you should also avoid joining agencies that are willing to ignore union-recommended rates of pay, doing 'deals' with film or TV production companies, offering SAs for cut-price rates in an effort to undercut their competition. You will end up working more hours for less money.

Legitimate agencies are expensive to run but, don't forget, they are also a business. It may not be in an up-front registration fee, but you will be expected to pay for their services somewhere along the line. Most agencies will charge a fee for your photo to go into their casting book. This book will be sent to all relevant production companies and may also be available on the Internet. The better companies will either not have this fee but ask you to supply and pay for your own photos, or will arrange for the photos to be taken, and then deduct the fee out of the wages for your first job. All agencies will also take a commission from payment for any work you do through them. Check what this commission rate is. The average is about fifteen per cent — any higher than this is unreasonable.

## HOW MANY AGENTS DO YOU NEED?

How many agencies you join really depends on how seriously you're going to take being an SA, and how often you expect to work. SA agencies will not demand exclusivity. There may be grudges between agencies, but don't listen to rumours about your agent not liking you being registered with another one. Some SAs join all the agencies they can, some stick to one or two — it's really up to you. Having more than one is a good way to judge between them though, as you can see for yourself the agents that offer the most work. If you are looking to work regularly, you do probably need to join at least two or three. Outside the London area you may not have the luxury of choice though, and there might only be one agency near you worth joining. Thankfully, agencies seem to be following the trend of not charging money from artistes up front. If you haven't paid anything up front to join an agency, it's obviously less risky to join more.

Before we look at the best way to apply, here's one person's experience of finding an agent:

I blame my wife. I had been a graphic designer for forty years and freelancing for thirty, but unavoidable changes in the business had led to a diminishing amount of work. Not only was I told to get off my backside and earn some money, but my ageing Porsche 924 also had to go! While leafing through *Loot* to determine its value, my wife spotted an ad for film and television Extras and photographic models, 'age/sex immaterial'. "You can do that," she said, "at least it will get you out of the house."

Next step was to call all the agencies listed in the London telephone book, to see who might take me on. I thought that being sixty-two and having no experience would be a problem, but photographic models (and particularly Supporting Artistes) are all ages, shapes and colours because they reflect reality: any magazine advertisement, film or television drama or soap will confirm this. I originally registered with several agencies on the grounds that one might be unable to provide as much work as I could handle, and I've joined more since. You soon find out which are best for you.

The question of costs is relevant here. Many agencies charge a fee (which varies) for inclusion on their website and/or in their casting book. Some don't levy a charge at all, and some will take their fees out of the first work they obtain for you. One of the first agencies I joined charges £50 a year, but soon after registering they found me six days' work on a BBC period drama series which more than compensated for the outlay. A clear case of having to speculate to accumulate!

Malcolm Lauder

## APPLYING

Prepare yourself for a shock. Because of the high level of applicants, any agent will probably look at the CV and photos that you have spent hours preparing for a maximum of twenty seconds. They will look at your photos for fifteen seconds and your CV for five. Having only twenty seconds to impress suggests you need to get this bit absolutely right if you are to be taken on.

### GETTING YOUR PHOTOS RIGHT

Here are some guidelines on how to present your photos:

**1** Supply two photos: one head-shot and one full-length. (Don't put in more than two, as they will probably end up in the bin.)

**2** Make sure they don't have sentimental value — they will not be returned to you.

**3** They must be recent photos, taken in the last month, and must convey how you currently look.

**4** Make sure they are big enough to get a good look at you, and are only of you, not group shots.

**5** Use colour rather than black and white.

**6** If you don't already have professional shots or cards, don't waste money getting them done.

If you supply a head-shot and a full-length photo you are covering all bases. It's a very quick way to see your body shape as opposed to just your face. Don't get paranoid about this; all body shapes and sizes are in demand. It's very important that your photos are recent. A person's appearance can change more quickly than you might imagine. If you don't think so, have a quick look at your photo album and compare two pictures of yourself taken a couple of years apart. If nothing else, your hair and possibly your weight will have changed. It sounds obvious to say that your photos need to show what you look like now, but there is nothing worse for an agent than seeing beautifully prepared photos that bear absolutely no resemblance to the person you later meet in the flesh. This can happen if an artiste has spent a lot of money having professional photos taken years ago and wants to get their money's worth, continuing to use them long past their 'sell-by date'!

Traditionally, prospective SAs would supply 'ten by eights' (the photos' size in inches). Some agencies will ask for professionally taken ten by eights, but most do not. Another format is the 'z card', a card with both photos and measurements (like fashion models use). Don't waste your money on either of these initially. Both are very expensive. If you want to be an actor or a professional model, you may need ten by eights or a card. But a lot of inexperienced SAs make the mistake of having these done up front, thinking it will increase their chances of being taken on by an agency. The reality is that it will not. While it's very important that they make the best possible impression, the photos you send in will not actually end up in the agency's casting book. If an agency takes you on, they will take their own photographs, or send you to their approved photographer.

Remember, the bigger the photos are, the better — passport photos are a definite no. If you've got a really flattering snap you want to use, get it reprinted, preferably a bit larger. Alternatively, get colour photocopies — a cheaper option if you are sending pictures out to lots of agencies. Colour photos are the preferred option because agents get a much better idea about skin tone. But if you already have really good quality black and white shots, use them.

Although technology has made it easy to send photos and CVs by email, it is better to send hard copies through the post. You may think that sending them by email puts you one step ahead, but the reality is actually the opposite. This is not because agents cannot cope with technology (although some are better than others). The problem is that you are relying on the agent to print them out at the other end. The quality of most office printers suggests that you will not look your best! Also, emails can get accidentally deleted or forgotten about at busy times. Make it easy for agents by having your photo and CV put straight in front of them — by post.

Despite not being looked at for long, your CV is important. Have a look at the sample CV and make sure yours has all the right components. The measurements you need to include are dependent on your sex. Height, hat size, shoe size, neck, chest and waist measurements are important for both sexes. Women should also include hip and dress sizes. Men should include inside leg. Although using feet and inches may not seem a very modern European approach, it is still the industry norm. Do not guess your sizes. If you do not know them, look at the labels in your clothing, get a tape measure out, and visit a hat shop for a fitting if necessary!

Keep experience relevant. Include what you are doing now, as well as any experience you have had working as an SA. If you don't have any SA experience, try to include something you have done that is comparable. If you have done any performance at all, be it theatre, amateur productions or even a stint as a wedding DJ, it's worth including as it shows you are confident. But be brief. Including part-time jobs you had when you left school may not be relevant if you're thirty-five.

The whole thing should be no longer than one side of A4 paper. If you do need more space, make it double sided, that way all the information about you is still on one sheet of paper. Some people like to include an introductory letter to give a bit of background. It's probably more concise to fit this on your CV if you can. It's a good idea to say something here about your availability. You should also list any relevant skills. When you make the list, ask yourself if you are likely to be asked to perform that skill on set, and only include things that you are confident enough to do in front of the camera. If it's something you haven't done in the last three years, forget it. Include any information about your personal wardrobe. It's useful for agents to know if you have a business suit or any formal wear, or if you have any types of uniform.

## CURRICULUM VITAE

**Name:** Jo Bright
**Skin tone:** white
**Age:** 49

**Home phone number:** 0201 5555 5555
**Mobile number:** 97944 555 555
**Email address:** jo.bright@com.com
**Contact Address:**
53 Road Street
London
W38 5PP

**Measurements (feet/inches):**
Height: 5/3
Hat Size: 7
Neck: 16
Chest: 36
Waist: 30
Hips: 40
Dress size: 12
Shoe size: 7

**Skills:** nurse, driving, juggler, ice skater, French speaker

**Wardrobe:** business suit, cocktail dress, formal evening wear, nurse's uniform.

**Introduction:**
I would like to introduce myself to your agency for consideration to go onto your books. I'm available to work at short notice as I'm currently not employed. I have a car and am good at getting around.

**Relevant experience:**
I once worked as an Extra on a production that was filming at my place of work and thoroughly enjoyed the experience. I am looking for a new part-time job, as my children have now left home. I am also a trained nurse.

Paperclip your CV to your photos or, even better, glue it to the back of one of them. Always include a stamped addressed envelope. Despite it being unlikely that your photos will be returned to you, it will encourage the agency to write to you. After you've done your research and sent off your applications, all you can do is sit back and wait. Don't hassle the agency by ringing them and asking if they have received your photos and CV. If you really want to be sure they get there, go to the post office and send your package by guaranteed delivery. If you are suitable, you will soon receive a response.

## THE INTERVIEW

Congratulations! You've sent out your photos and CVs, and an agency has contacted you — they're interested in taking you on. What happens next? Most agencies will call you in for an informal interview before they put you on their books. The idea behind this process is simply to assess your suitability in person. It's a good idea to take another copy of your CV with you, and have to hand details of any relevant skills and wardrobe you might have. If the agency wants to take their own photos at the same time as the interview (which is often the case), find out what they'd like you to wear. Remember that those making the casting decisions will be judging you on these photos — in the agency's book — for at least a year. Try not to make too much of a 'statement' with what you are wearing — you are trying to make yourself look suitable for as much work as possible, so neutral clothing is important. Generally it's a good idea to dress smarter, as it's easier for someone to imagine you more casual than to imagine you in smart clothes. The exception to this is if you are an 'extraordinary' type. If you expect to get most of your work because you are a punk, don't go dressed in a suit.

## WHAT TO WEAR

Individual agencies will give you their own guidelines on what to wear for their photos, but here are some general rules to follow:

**1** Wear solid colours rather than patterns.

**2** Do not wear anything with large logos or pictures. It will distract from your face.

**3** Avoid bright colours; mid-tone colours usually photograph better. All white or all black will not photograph well.

**4** Wear clothing that is flattering and makes you feel comfortable and confident. If you feel good, you will be more at ease with the photographer.

**5** Be prepared, you may not have that much time to get ready. Men should be clean-shaven (ie, no stubble, unless otherwise instructed; beards and moustaches are fine unless, again, otherwise instructed); women should have completed hair and make-up on arrival. You will only get a minute or two, just enough time to check yourself in the mirror, before you start.

## CONTRACTS

Whilst working as an SA there are two main types of contract that you will encounter. Firstly there is an agency agreement. When you do manage to register with an agent, you will be asked to sign an agency agreement, or Terms and Conditions. Make sure you read this carefully and get a copy for future reference. This will detail any fees and commission you will pay the agency, and will lay out the arrangement between you the artiste, any production company you work for, and the agency. If you're not asked to sign such a contract, beware — it may suggest a badly run agency that could change its commission rates or fees at any time. This contract should also make reference to the length of time it takes for you to be paid. The law dictates that the agency pays you within ten days of them receiving the money from the production company. For more details of what to expect, there's a sample agency contract on page 133.

The second type of contract you will encounter is a release form. Whatever you work on, the production company is your employer, not the agency. This release form details the specific arrangement between that production company and you as the artiste. The production company also needs this for insurance. In reality these forms are nearly always standard, but make sure you read each one you receive carefully. On film and TV sets you will normally receive a salary voucher (or 'chit', as they are sometimes referred to). On this form will be detailed any amounts of pay that you accumulate during the day, but these vouchers will always also contain a standard release. You are basically signing away your rights over how your image and voice appear on the screen. The list below gives more details; see also the sample salary voucher/release form on pages 131-132.

### WHAT TO EXPECT ON A STANDARD RELEASE FORM

The standard release will normally contain the following:

1 Your consent for your voice and image to be used, either in a motion picture, photography or sound recording. (And consent for your voice to be dubbed into any language.)

2 Your acknowledgement that this is a buyout of your rights

and that this image can be used 'throughout the world in perpetuity'.

**3** The consent also extends to any advertising, publicity or merchandise in connection to the production.

**4** A reference to the 1988 Copyright, Designs and Patent Act.

Some release forms will also contain:

**5** Acknowledgement that you cannot disclose any confidential material to the media about the production, or take photographs on set.

**6** Confirmation that you are a British citizen, member of the EU or Commonwealth.

## GETTING YOUR FIRST JOB

So, you're on an agency's books and eager to work. Chapter 3 looks in detail at the process of casting, and getting ready for a day on set, but how do you get to that stage? Knowing what is currently in production doesn't necessarily help you to get any more jobs. But it can be a good idea to try and find out how much filming there is going on, or coming up, in your area, and whether it's a busy period or not — if only so you know what you might be asked to work on, and when. Once you start getting work, and are on set, you will hear artistes talking about other upcoming or in-progress productions, but getting that first job might take some time, so be prepared for a wait.

Becoming known to your agent personally amongst the sea of other faces is your biggest challenge. This may take a while, but it will be much more to your benefit to be known as a polite, friendly person, as opposed to a troublemaker, or someone who hassles the agents. It can take several months to receive your first call, but — as I've said before and will say again — patience is a vital attribute when working as an SA.

What kind of production might your first job be on? Many new SAs are eager to work on the TV soaps, figuring that, as they film all year round, demand for Extras must be huge. The main soaps are:

*EastEnders* and *Family Affairs* in London, *Coronation Street* in Manchester, *Hollyoaks* in Chester, *Brookside* in Liverpool and *Emmerdale* in Leeds. Then there are a few TV dramas that are nearly always in production, such as *The Bill* and *London's Burning* in London and *Casualty* in Bristol. However, all of these programmes tend to have regular SAs who appear in episode after episode — and not many of them at that, so competition to get work on these shows is fierce. The reason for the limited numbers is that the action in soaps tends to focus around a few particular locations. Think of *EastEnders*: there's the café, the laundrette, the pub and the Square; for added realism it makes sense to see familiar faces in the background, rather than a completely different bunch of people in every episode. (For example, you might not have noticed it consciously, but the same Supporting Artiste has actually been playing Albert Square's milkman for years!)

You are therefore more likely to be offered your first job on a big crowd scene in a movie or TV drama. The Internet can be a useful source of information about what productions are filming, or are in pre-production. There are lots of rumour sites, which if you have an interest in the movies are fascinating in their own right (you can find a list of them at the back of the book), but remember, rumours are rumours, and the information can be fairly unreliable. For a reliable round-up of what's in production and pre-production, get hold of a copy of the industry trade papers *Screen International* (for films) or *Broadcast* (for TV productions). You can buy or order these from bigger newsagents, or find them in the library. BECTU also produces a quarterly bulletin called *Early Bird*. This details upcoming productions, but you have to be a member to get hold of it.

Finding out what commercials and pop videos are in production is trickier. These happen so quickly (often shooting for just a day) it would be a full-time job tracking them. But as a general rule, ninety per cent of commercials and pop videos are filmed in the London area. (Chapter 8 looks at what is filmed in other regions of the UK in more detail.)

Some people can be very sensitive if they're not working, becoming paranoid that they are the only one without a steady stream of jobs, particularly if their fellow SAs seem busier. Do not fall into the trap of thinking you are going to be suitable for every job that comes along. In the days of the closed shop, the attitude was that any SA was suitable for anything, and everyone was interchangeable. Today, this could not be further from the truth. Start with the attitude that if you don't look right, you will not be used. If your agency is worth its salt, it will only suggest people to the production company who are absolutely right for the role, and fit the brief it has been given exactly. It's good to be aware of what's filming, or is due to start filming, but don't push your luck: I know of one particular 'professional' SA who keeps a notebook of which agencies are casting whatever is currently in production. He then phones up each one and demands work: "You're doing such and such aren't you? I haven't been on that yet." Any agent will tell you that this is *incredibly* annoying. Trust that your agent knows what they're doing, and if you are suitable, you will be called.

## CAREER OR HOBBY — 'PROFESSIONAL' VS DAY PLAYER

It's worth taking a moment at this point to discuss being a full-time SA. After your first few successful assignments you may think you've found your new career. Beware! A common question for an agent to hear is, "I've been thinking about giving up my full-time job. Will you be able to give me enough work?" This is an impossible question to answer, since the agent will probably only have an idea of what is filming in the next one to three months. Think very carefully; do not hand in your resignation just yet.

The way you view background work will completely depend on your outlook on life. Traditionally, those in related industries such as the theatre, or cabaret singers, used to work as SAs in quiet times to help pay the bills. Because it was a closed shop, non-industry people rarely got a look in. Today things are different. It still remains the case that for most artistes SA work is not their only source of income, but today SAs come from all walks of life. But remember, very few people survive by working as an SA full time.

Just because you've been busy for a while doesn't necessarily mean you will continue to be. Make a list of what you have worked on. Has it been one production, or have you been used on lots of different ones? For the HBO Second World War TV series *Band of Brothers*, a large number of men who resembled soldiers were used as SAs. Nearly 1,000 of them worked on the miniseries for the nine months it filmed in Hatfield. Some were caught out when filming finished. They had given up their previous jobs, and had been working for up to five days a week as Second World War soldiers. When production stopped, so did the regular work; they had wrongly assumed that long runs of work were the norm. It's important to remember the roller-coaster effect. When it's quiet, you don't want to find yourself struggling to pay the bills.

Make sure you have a back-up plan. View SA work as a supplement to your main income, not the other way round. This attitude will take the pressure off finding work in quiet times.

If, looking at your list, you find you've been used on many different jobs given by different agents, you may be one of the lucky 'ordinary' types whose face seems to fit most things. Even so, be very careful about giving up any other income. It is a big risk if things suddenly go quiet. Getting the combination right between your work on set and any other income can be a tricky balance, and usually takes a couple of years to work out.

The word 'professional' has, in some circles, become a dirty word in connection with Supporting Artistes. Saying you are a professional and conducting yourself professionally on set are not always the same thing, and can indeed sometimes be opposites. If you start work as an SA, try to avoid falling into the two-tiered snobbery of the professional versus the 'day player'. Remember that this industry needs new faces to survive. If the same people appeared in the background of our screens all the time it would be very dull to watch! That is not to say that we don't need professionals, as learning from their experience can be very important for newcomers. The structure of the filming process is a natural hierarchy. At the top is the Director and Producer and, some would say, at the bottom are the Supporting Artistes. It seems to be part of the culture that some professional SAs adopt this hierarchy, and start to look down on the new recruits. This is a mistake. Stick together and try to help those who are not certain of what they're doing, rather than sneering at them. Remember how you felt on your first job. Whilst working as an SA you are part of a very large team, and it's important to keep that in mind.

So, it's important to approach the idea with caution, but 'going pro' does work for some SAs, especially if they manage to go beyond background work to Walk-on parts, and longer-term jobs as actors' Stand-ins — both of these types of jobs and more are covered in Chapter 7. To end this chapter though, here's one artiste's take on going full-time:

Going full-time as a Supporting Artiste or Stand-in can be a scary move. I went for it because I was sick of nine-to-five, same place every day, routine-type jobs which were making me miserable. I had tried office jobs and working in retail, and I couldn't hack it. So I quit.

It felt like stepping into a void, but free-falling can be fun. Plus, I love films and film sets, where nothing is ever routine and you're never quite sure what to expect. Even in my worst moments in background work, I would rather be doing that than any previous job I've had.

The main risk in becoming full-time is that there will not be enough work. This is a very real possibility, and I have used temp agencies to get me through the quiet patches. Being a Stand-in allows for longer runs of work, which in turn generate enough income to keep me going through the gaps in between jobs. It would be great to be established enough that I could go from job to job, but that is a lifestyle reserved for very few.

Another drawback is that you become scared to turn down work, or plan anything else in case you miss out on a job. Also, it can be extremely frustrating when jobs clash (I always end up convincing myself that I took the wrong one), but then there are the times when I'm glad that I took every job going, because the work has suddenly dried up and I have to fall back on my savings. The flip side of the unpredictable nature of this industry is the versatility and freedom it allows you, and the refreshing lack of routine and constraints. Scary for some, exhilarating for others.

**Bella Sabbagh**

# CASTING

For some Supporting Artistes, exactly how casting decisions are made within an agency can be a bit of a mystery, as they feel a little 'out of the loop'. The aim of this chapter is to give you a greater insight into how agencies work, suggesting things you can do to make yourself more appealing to agents, and therefore ensure that you maximize your potential.

## INSIDE THE AGENCY

Typically, your agency will be made up of a number of agents, strictly called Casting Co-ordinators, but also referred to in the industry (and in this book) as 'Bookers'. Depending on the agency's size the number of Bookers can range from one to five, plus additional support staff — usually at least one accountant, to deal with your payments. Different agencies work in different ways, but it is normal for each Booker to have individual projects that they manage and co-ordinate with the relevant production company. Some Bookers may specialise in partic-ular types of work: one may deal with commercials, one with pop videos and so on. Generally they all work independently, but help each other manage the high levels of phone calls that are involved.

For commercials, pop videos and photographic casting briefs, the Casting Director involved will normally approach several agencies. For TV and film productions, it's the Assistant Director's (or 2nd AD's) role to cast the Extras, and one agency tends to get a contract to sup-ply all the SAs needed. How an agency gets those contracts is some-thing of a black art. It's pretty much a buyer's market these days, and competition between agencies to win contracts can be fierce. Some desperate, less professional agents have been known to try bribery or backhanders, from sending Assistant Directors gifts, to offering to pay back to the production company, under the table, part of the commission it would earn in an attempt to secure the contract. Thankfully none of these underhand methods work, as ultimately who gets the job is dependent on one thing — the company's reputation.

An agency's reputation is made up of three components: firstly, how good the agency staff are at casting and co-ordinating the right people for the job; secondly, what projects they have worked on before; and thirdly, but most importantly, the calibre of the artistes on their books. Within the industry there are only a small number of Assistant Directors and Casting Directors who decide which agency to use for which production. Word of mouth can work for or against an agency; in the same way that artistes talk to each other, production crews will also discuss which are the good agencies and which are not.

Generally ADs find an agency that works well for them, and then tend to stick to that winning formula. Remember it's their job on the line if the SAs are wrong, so trust plays a big part between the Bookers and the production team. For this reason, if you do something wrong as an SA you will probably get a good telling-off from your agent — after all, whether the agency keeps a contract is partly dependent on how reliable and well behaved their artistes are. One thing is certain: if there are problems, that agency will not be used again by that Assistant Director, so the Bookers are working under a lot of pressure to get the casting absolutely right.

## THE CASTING PROCESS

There are two methods of casting SAs: casting from photos, and calling artistes to a casting to see them in the flesh. Casting from photos is the normal method, but for featured roles or Walk-ons you may be asked to attend a casting.

Assistant Directors tend to fall into three main camps in terms of how they work with the agency Booker. Some like to keep complete control of the casting process and will go through the casting books themselves to pick SAs they would like to use (this route is more likely if a production has appointed a separate Crowd Assistant Director). Other ADs have built up a good working relationship with the Bookers, and trust them to book the SAs 'sight unseen'. On a feature film or television drama, the Booker will then effectively become part of the crew, and will be given the script to read, to give them a mental picture of how the production is going to look. They will also be given a breakdown of the entire filming period, split into filming days, with notes of what is required in each scene. The third way is a combination of both methods and is more tightly controlled by the AD, who allows the Booker to make the casting decisions, but only lets them know what they need day-by-day. This could be more common on a soap opera.

These three approaches are not set in stone, and some ADs may employ a combination of methods. They may leave the background casting in the hands of the Booker, but become more involved with featured roles and Walk-ons. For these roles the Booker might make suggestions from the casting book, and the Assistant Director may then show these to the Director to decide which artiste to choose. Occasionally the Director may want to meet the shortlisted artistes in person to make a final decision.

## GOING TO A CASTING

Other types of jobs, such as commercials, pop videos and photographic shoots, can be cast straight from photos, but often you will be asked to go to a casting so you can be seen in person. The process goes like this: Casting Directors send out briefs to multiple agencies. The Bookers then contact SAs who they think match the brief, and check their availability. The Casting Director then checks the suggested SAs' photos in the book to see if they agree that the choices match the brief, and will select any that they think are suitable. The Booker then sends the selected artistes to the casting. The turnaround for this process is very fast; normally the agency only gets these briefs the day before the casting.

The drawback with castings is that you will not normally be paid to attend. It can seem fairly hit or miss, and often is. For example, if the brief is for only one role (which they often are), it might have been sent to five different agencies and each one sends perhaps five people, meaning that you've only got a one in twenty-five chance of being selected. The reason artistes take the trouble to go to such castings is simple: if they *are* selected, the financial rewards are much higher. Traditionally, if an artiste had a featured role in a commercial, repeat fees would be paid every time the commercial was shown. In today's digital multi-channel environment, artistes are more often than not offered an up-front, lump sum 'buyout' from these repeat fees. Depending on the usage of the commercial (how often it is shown, and on which channels), this can run into thousands of pounds.

Castings are also more common if you are required to perform any type of creative reaction; productions don't want SAs who look great in the book photo but stand like a stone statue in the flesh! The normal scenario will be that the Casting Director or AD will give you a situation and ask you to act it out, or they may ask you to read from a script. (More advice on how to behave in these kinds of castings can be found in Chapter 7.) Sometimes you may turn up at the casting and all that happens is a Polaroid is taken of you. This may seem a little pointless, but it stems from a mistrust of the photo of you in the book. Occasionally the same artiste may look completely different in two different agency books.

You may be asked to go to the casting dressed in a particular way. What you are asked to wear will help create the right image. A Polaroid of you in a particular costume, such as a cocktail dress, may help the Director to see your potential more than a photo in a casting book of you wearing a T-shirt and jeans. When the stakes are high, a Casting Director may feel they need to be absolutely sure they pick the right person, so meeting you in the flesh, in costume, will help them.

Because of the large number of people going to castings it is quite common not to get any immediate feedback. Artistes often phone their agent, asking if they have any news. Unless you have been offered another job and need to know about a specific day, there is little point in doing this. It's better to assume that if you haven't heard anything, your agent hasn't heard either. It can be several days after the casting before the agency is told who has been picked. If you have been selected your agent will obviously call you straight away.

## BEFORE THE FILMING DAY

Productions that require Supporting Artistes can be divided into three main types: contemporary or present-day, fantasy or futuristic and period productions.

Some jobs will require you to go to a fitting *before* the filming day (it's usually not on the filming day itself because of time restrictions). You will however normally be paid for this, and you should allow at least four hours once you've arrived to complete your fitting.

## TYPES OF FITTINGS

**Costume Fitting:** This is more common on — but not exclusive to — period and fantasy productions. You may need to go for a costume fitting on present-day productions if you require a uniform or special clothing. For example, in *Notting Hill*, the posh restaurant scenes required a *maître d'*, some waiters, guests in formal evening wear and doormen, all of whom were fitted before filming. Sometimes you may attend a 'show and tell' fitting. For this you will be asked to take along your own clothing, for example a tuxedo, and the costume department will use this as a starting point, sometimes not changing you at all, or maybe adding things to what you have, and occasionally changing you into something else altogether.

**Prosthetics Fitting:** Sometimes a production (usually fantasy or futuristic ones) will need to change your appearance, and you will be fitted for a prosthetic make-up appliance. On the *Harry Potter* films for example, witches need to have longer noses and bigger chins. On *Gladiator*, amputees were hired as SAs, and were fitted for false legs or arms, which were specially made so they could then be chopped off in battle!

**Body Cast:** This involves making a mould of your body shape, or a part of your body. It is less common than prosthetics, but for example in *The Mummy*, some SAs were dressed up as Mummies and needed to get body casts before their costumes could be made.

**Haircut:** Depending on the time period in which the film is set, you may require a haircut. This is more likely if hair needs to be particularly tidy. This may be done on the day, but will sometimes be done in advance. Occasionally you may be asked to go to a wig fitting, particularly if you are doubling an actor (see Chapter 7 for more on doubling).

## THE BOOKING

There is a fairly set procedure to any booking. Firstly you will receive a call from your Booker to check your availability on a particular day, or number of dates. On big productions the Bookers will normally be organising each scene about a week before filming. However, with last-minute changes inevitable, you might be receiving calls up until the day before shooting. Make sure you always carry a pocket diary and pencil with you (they're as essential for any SA as a mobile phone) — if dates start to move about, it can get confusing and you don't want to get bookings mixed up. You must *always* write down the name of the production, which Booker you spoke to about the job, which agency the booking is for, and the status of the booking (see below). If you are not told any of this information, make sure you ask. If you have to call back with a query about a booking it can be a bit embarrassing if you can't remember the name of the production or who booked you for it!

## THE STATUS OF YOUR BOOKING

It's important for you to gauge the likelihood of this booking happening. There are four types of status that are often referred to by your Booker:

**Light Pencil:** Usually meaning the date could change.

**Pencil:** This is just as important to you as a confirmed booking. Keep this day free and do not take another job on this date without first checking with your agent to see if they can release you.

**Heavy Pencil:** More often used for features or Walk-ons. Possibly the Director hasn't decided yet who to pick from a shortlist, normally of two or three artistes.

**Confirmed Booking:** Filming should happen on that day, but remember that things can still change at short notice.

You may be given your call time and location when you're booked for a job. More likely you will be asked to call the agency back at a given time to get these details — this is normally the afternoon of the day before filming. When you do pick up your details, there is a checklist of information you must make sure you are given:

### YOUR BOOKING: WHAT YOU NEED TO KNOW

**1** An exact location and a precise time at which to be there. ☐

**2** The name of the contact you will be meeting. ☐

**3** An emergency number in case something goes wrong. This number may be of a production person who will be at the location, or it may be for someone from the agency. ☐

**4** Any wardrobe requirements. ☐

Knowing about wardrobe requirements is very important. If the production is present-day and you are not being fitted in a costume, you may be given strict instructions on certain colours to avoid wearing, or told whether they want you to dress in a particular way, for example casual or in a suit. As a general rule you should always avoid wearing anything too distracting. This means no really bright colours and nothing that has large logos or pictures.

If you are working on a night shoot, be careful about booking yourself on another job earlier that day, or on the following day. Some artistes do manage it, but working all night and then all day is very exhausting and can be dangerous if you are driving. It is tempting to keep going for the money, but the second production will not thank you for turning up late, and being useless because you are too tired. Doing this is also a gamble because the chances are that at the time of the booking, you won't know when the night shoot will finish and what time the day shoot will be called, or vice versa, so it's possible you could be expected to be in two places at once.

## CANCELLATIONS

As you have almost certainly gathered by now, the nature of filming is that schedules change, often at very short notice. This may be because an actor is unwell or the weather is wrong, or it could just be that filming has fallen behind schedule. It is accepted industry practice that a 'confirmed' booking can be cancelled by the production right up until 5.30pm the day before filming. The agency is duty bound to try and get a message to you as soon as they know a booking has been cancelled. If the production company has called off your job after 5.30pm, you may be entitled to a cancellation fee, which is normally the flat daily rate. Your agent will tell you if you are entitled to this. Because filming can be seven days a week, there is no difference to this rule at weekends, so if you are cancelled over the weekend for a Monday you will not be entitled to a cancellation fee, unless it is later than 5.30pm on the Sunday night. A job being cancelled at the last minute is something most SAs get to experience. It can however be worse for some than for others...

The call came in at about 4pm and was nothing less than a miracle. I hadn't worked since the costly loss of my stick-on moustache on the set of *The End of the Affair*. The agency told me I had been selected to double as a young version of Michael Caine's character on the film *Last Orders*, and it was a week's work too. I was chuffed, as doubling kind of makes you feel like a real star and I've always been a big Caine fan. I was utterly perplexed though as to how on earth they had chosen me for the job — with my dark brown hair and eyes, I wasn't exactly Caine's colouring. "No matter," said the agency. "A wig?" I asked. "Not quite," they said. It was then that the full horror of the job materialised. For in order to secure the gig I would have to dye my hair ginger, and in order to get my hair ginger, I would first have to bleach it white.

I was desperate for money though, and to get back onto a film set, so with my last £30 I booked myself in and endured three hours of scalp-burning chemicals, and then a bottle of permanent dye. There I was, as ginger as one could be. Still, I thought, it could be worse — it could be natural. It was at around 8pm that I received another call. It was the agency again. "Don't worry about that job anymore Jos, it's been cancelled." And there you have it: I was skint, jobless and ginger. In my eyes the whole industry had become, quite literally, discoloured!

Jos Dewing

## INCREASING YOUR CHANCES OF BEING BOOKED

It is difficult to influence those who make the casting decisions (see Chapter 7 for suggestions), but there are a few important attributes you can demonstrate to help you get picked more often by Bookers.

Most importantly, be reliable. You will probably not be given a second chance if you don't turn up for a job without at least letting your agent know there is a problem. Remember, if you do drop out, the Booker has to replace you, sometimes out of office hours late at night or early in the morning. If you seem to be letting them down a lot, they simply won't use you again. If you have to lie your way out of a situation, all I can say is: don't get caught doing it. An artiste once phoned to let us know he hadn't made it to a very important job because that morning his wife had gone into labour and had just had her baby. Congratulations were offered and the incident was forgotten. The problem arose when three months later he rang again and said exactly the same thing.

Be polite and friendly and try not to be a nuisance to your agent. It's not unusual for a Booker to get 100 calls a day, and at busy times this can double. So try to help them by being brief and well organised. If you have to keep phoning back and checking details, this will become wearing. Don't ask questions that the agent doesn't know the answer to. The worst offender for this is, "What time will it finish?" Not even the Director knows the answer to this! Also, try not to call the Booker on their mobile in the evenings or at weekends unless it is essential. If your query can wait until the next day, leave it until then.

Do not be late for jobs; timekeeping is one of the most important attributes you can keep control over. Those who get a reputation for always being late will not be the agent's first choice. Similarly if you are told to call back at a set time to pick up details of a job, make sure you do. It can be annoying if the agency has to chase up artistes at the end of the day because they have not called in when they were told to. Do not phone up and 'check in' for work unless you know you're allowed to. Some agencies require you to check in and let them know your availability, but most do not. Artistes who constantly check in for jobs will become an irritation, as such calls generally stop the Bookers from actually doing their work. Find out what your agency's policy is; some allow you to do it at certain times, some don't allow you to check in at all.

Never use emotional blackmail to try and get more work. It's amazing how often people say, "Have I done something to upset you?" to their agent — there is nothing more upsetting to the Booker than hearing that line. If you haven't heard from your agency for a long while, give them a quick call and tell them that *politely*. Trying to make them feel responsible for how you are going to feed yourself or pay the rent this month will not be well received. That's the agent's viewpoint; however here's an example of what it can be like at the other end of the phone:

The knowledge that there are jobs out there and you're not getting them makes it difficult to resist the urge to phone up every day or so, just to remind your agents that you're alive. I used to be with an agency that suggested its clients phone in every day. At first this seemed to me to be a great way to assuage my anxiety over being forgotten, but when you hear the same voice saying, "No, nothing today," and slamming the phone down (their people skills could have used a little work) on a regular basis, it becomes more disheartening than hearing nothing at all. On the whole, I get enough unprompted calls to reassure me that I've not been forgotten (though not, of course, as many as I'd like), but on the occasions when I phone in and am immediately offered work, I do wonder whether it was coincidence or consequence! The bottom line is: it is never a good idea to make an enemy of your agent. They are not spiteful people (at least, not the ones I've met) and will do their best to find the right person for the right job. Nagging them will do no one any favours and will eventually result in less work for you.

**Bella Sabbagh**

When you do get a call, make sure you do not accidentally double book yourself on more than one job on the same day. If schedules change and filming dates are moving, it can be easy to make a mistake, particularly if you have more than one agent. This is why you should always check your diary before accepting a job. If you are not sure about a date, check it and then ring your agent back. This will be appreciated much more than accepting a job and then ringing back to say you are not available. If you are asked to go to a casting, make sure you find out what the filming dates will be if you are selected. It would be a huge waste of everyone's time if you are picked, and then not available for the shoot.

Keep your perspective. If you are doing well and frequently getting Walk-ons and featured roles, be careful about suddenly dumping normal background work. Another cliché often used by artistes is, "I'm features only now." Your agent is not in the business of holding you back, but it can be quite frustrating for an agency to have artistes that refuse to do background work. If you feel that way, it may be time to consider looking for an acting agent (see Chapter 7). Don't forget that for Bookers, the really useful artistes are the ones who can do features and Walk-ons, but don't mind doing background work as well.

Finally, behave yourself on set. If a bad report comes back against you, the chances are this will damage your reputation with the agency and possibly stop you being booked for work altogether. Of course, sometimes it may not be your fault. If that is the case but you suspect something might be said against you, phone up your agency and let them know your side of the story first. Agents have heard everything, and if they believe you have been mistreated, they won't hold a bad report against you. Occasionally, on-set disputes happen, but never try to battle it out alone. If you are having a problem, phone your agent and get them to deal with it. If you stick to these suggestions, you will soon become known as a reliable artiste and, if you are suitable for something, your agent will not hesitate to book you.

# THE FILMING DAY

After sending off your CV and photos, registering with your agents and spending weeks or months waiting by the phone for a call, you've finally been booked for your first job — and you're due on set the next day. There are lots of different types of productions you could be asked to work on (more detail can be found in Chapter 5), but as a case study we will examine the process of working as an SA on a feature film, from the night before to the end of the filming day.

## BE PREPARED

It is often said that one of the toughest parts of doing background work is getting out of bed. It is normal for your call time on set to be 7am, and this often means getting up at 5am, or earlier if it's a particularly remote location. Worst case, it is not uncommon to have an on set call time as early as 4.30am. The key to arriving on time is planning the night before. Look up on a map *exactly* where you have to be. Plan your route carefully. If you cannot find it on a map, do something about it. Do not leave it until the morning. The Internet has some useful sites that will help when planning a route, and a list of these can be found at the back of this book. You may be going to a film studio, such as Pinewood or Shepperton. It's a good idea to familiarise yourself with where the main studios are (again, there's a list of addresses at the back of the book).

## THE NIGHT BEFORE

Many SAs do not sleep well the night before a shoot because they worry about oversleeping. So what can you do to make sure you get out of bed on time? A good tip is to use two alarm clocks, positioning one far enough away that you actually have to get out of bed to turn it off!

Getting up may sound easy, but once you start to work a few days in a row (as is often the case with big crowd scenes) and you have not made it back to bed until late, your body will start to reject the idea of getting up at 4am. Do not make things harder for yourself by going out the night before. And if you are working on a night shoot, make sure you have had plenty of rest during the day. You don't want to find yourself dozing off in the middle of a take...

When using public transport, make sure you know which bus or train you are catching, and have a back-up plan in case something goes wrong. Keep a few taxi numbers in your diary. Resorting to a cab is a good option if your train is delayed or cancelled. This may be expensive, but the last thing you want to do is be late. If you have a journey by car, make sure you have enough petrol. Try to find out before you set off where you are going to park and how long the journey is going to take. Always overestimate your journey time. If you think it will take an hour, allow an hour and a half. Being early is always looked upon favourably.

Make sure you know exactly where you will be reporting. If you are filming at a studio, you have to know where in the studio complex you need to report (they're big places!). If the production is filming on location, you will probably be reporting at one of two places: the unit base or the location. These are fairly self-explanatory: the unit base is where the filming unit have set up base for the day, with all their vehicles and trailers, and the location is where the actual filming is happening. Although normally close, the two are not always in the same place and could be a mile apart, so going to the wrong one will obviously make you late. On bigger calls there may be a third meeting point — the crowd base, which may not be in the same place as the unit base. Knowing these little things in advance will help make that feeling of being up at 5am a little less painful.

Most SAs have their very own 'getting to the set on time' stories. Here are a few for you to learn from:

> Background work is definitely not for the lie-in-bed. Most Supporting Artistes are organisational geniuses with a talent that would have outdone Napoleon and all his generals. I always get ready the night before, my bags packed with essentials: thermals, crossword book, pen, NI number, toilet paper (for crowd scenes), invisible make-up (for costume drama) and indigestion tablets.

Clothes for travelling are laid in a trail from where I fall out of bed until I reach the front door. Early morning calls can be tricky in that you lay awake all night worrying that you may not wake up on time, only to find that you've fallen asleep just minutes before the alarm rings!

Even if you are armed with the A-Z of London and an Ordnance Survey Map of Great Britain, with an optional Auto-route programmed into your computer, it's still a good idea (trust me) to work out your route the day before and *not* leave it to chance. It's a known fact that although "all roads lead to Rome", in the film business "all signs lead *from* London", so if you live outside of the city, route instructions have to be worked backwards. Driving through the countryside in the early hours of the morning looking for the film unit's signs to the location in your wing mirrors is not an easy feat.

One-way systems are a nightmare, *especially* if you're working on *Casualty* in Bristol, where there aren't any unit signs. Some friends of mine once travelled down to Bristol looking for the industrial estate where *Casualty* is filmed and ended up outside the wrong warehouse, being given a guided tour by an estate agent after being mistaken for prospective buyers. It was only the lack of the tea/coffee stand that alerted them to this misunderstanding.

**Sue Hallet**

---

No problem, I thought, upon discovering that my alarm clock was broken. For the first time, I set the alarm on my mobile phone instead and left it next to the bed, confident that I would be awoken at five on Saturday morning. Imagine my horror when I awoke to the radio playing — my husband's alarm. I knew it was set for six and that I should have already left home for the tube station. I was ready to leave in ten minutes (as I always have everything prepared the night before), by which time my husband (bless him!) had volunteered to drive me up to London. Why hadn't my mobile alarm gone off? Because although I had set the alarm, I hadn't set the date and time correctly on the phone. Needless to say I always remember to check both now.

It was like *Planes, Trains and Automobiles* trying to get to the location, as neither of us knew how to get from the City to Regent's

Park. The whole way I was simultaneously applying make-up, checking the A-Z and debating whether and where to get out to catch a tube to make up for lost time. Eventually I spotted a black cab for hire in Trafalgar Square, jumped out of the car and into the cab and got to the location with seconds to spare... The 2nd AD wondered why I was there so early. The night before she had changed the call time to an hour and a half later but the message had never got through to the agency, or me!

**Stephanie Barrows**

---

If you have an early start on a shoot, I'd advise attaching two rather large alarm clocks to your ears, as it is vital to be on time for a production. If not, you'll be faced with an angry Director (believe me, they're scary!) and the worst costume on set as punishment!

I was doing a shoot for *London's Burning*, which involved a 6am start on location in London. Knowing how important it is to be on time, and how far away I live from London (in deepest darkest Kent), I still forgot to set my alarm clock and woke up at 5.30am with a bad hair day and no idea how to get to the location. In my panic I called the Production Manager who advised me that a team of hired ambulances were coming up from Brighton through my neighbourhood on their way to the shoot. Perfect!

I certainly travelled in style that day, lying on a stretcher in the back of an ambulance hurtling up the A2 with the siren flashing, but you can't always rely on the emergency services to get you there on time. So my advice is always plan your route well in advance, get a friend to phone you to make sure you get up on time, and failing that always make friends with the paramedics on set – I even got a lift home!

**Lucy Wallis**

## WHAT NOT TO TAKE

Personal cameras are strictly forbidden on sets. On big films you can get into a lot of trouble by taking pictures. Whilst shooting a sequence in the UK for the latest *Star Wars* movie, *Attack of the Clones*, all the SAs were replaced, and told never to come back — because one of them had apparently taken a photograph of a costume and tried to sell it to a newspaper. In the end it turned out it wasn't one of the SAs at all, but just the possibility that it might have been was enough for a few people to have their dream of being in *Star Wars* shattered. This is an extreme example, but be aware that at the very least, being seen with a camera will probably result in it being taken away from you.

A switched on mobile phone should never be taken on set. This is not to say that you can't have your phone with you. On route to a job they are essential if you have a problem. However, when you arrive on set make sure it is switched *off*. Use your phone only during a break, away from the filming area. God help you if your phone goes off during a take. Also, don't take anything valuable, such as your best watch or jewellery. If you're in costume, you'll have to leave all your belongings behind in the wardrobe department, where they will not be secure.

## WHAT TO TAKE

If you are making your own way, make sure you take a good map or A-Z with you. You might think you know where you're going, but if you get lost early in the morning there may not be anyone around to ask for directions. With filming being ten per cent action and ninety per cent waiting around, it is a very good idea to take something that can occupy your time. A good book or newspaper is obvious; the well prepared arrive with pocket chess and backgammon sets!

Depending on the time of year and the type of scene, you might want to carefully consider your underwear. Thermal long johns have saved many dressed as soldiers from the long hours in the cold, and from itchy woollen costumes. Even on present-day scenes, think beforehand if you are likely to be outside. British weather is unpredictable, so a warm coat is essential and it's a good idea to keep an umbrella in the car. If you know you are filming outside, check the weather forecast before you set out. Remember that you could be on your feet all day, so make sure you have comfortable shoes.

The wardrobe department will not always provide costumes. Sometimes you will be asked to take a selection of your own clothes. Normally you will get a wardrobe brief when you call in for your details, or the wardrobe department may phone you separately to advise you what to take. There are some general rules that will help you. Avoid very bright colours; you are in the background so you do not want to draw attention to yourself. Unless you are otherwise instructed, the main colours to avoid are whites and reds. Large logos are a definite no. Companies pay big money for product placement in a film — free advertising will not be allowed! It's also worth noting that checks and fine lines on clothing can cause problems when seen close up on camera. There are certain types of wardrobe requirement that are asked for again and again (evening wear, business suits etc), and owning them will increase your chances of being offered work. (For more advice on this, see Chapter 7.)

Finally, it's worth having a pen on you, so you will be able to fill in the paperwork on arrival. Also — as always — keep your pocket diary with you. During breaks you may pick up messages regarding other bookings. Often if an agent can't get a definite yes from you, they may be under pressure to book someone else. You don't want to miss work because you haven't got your diary on you to check your availability.

## GETTING THERE

Sometimes on bigger productions a coach may be provided to the location. You will be given a central rendezvous point and a specific time at which to meet the coach. If you are told that the pick-up time is 7am, allow yourself at least an additional fifteen minutes, making sure you arrive at 6.45am at the latest. The coach will not wait for you, and over-keen drivers have been known to leave five minutes early.

If you are making your own way, a good tip is to look out for the unit signs. You may have seen these around. Usually brightly coloured arrows tied to lampposts, they are temporary signs put up the day before by the location department, to help the crew find their way. They may say 'Unit' for unit base or 'Loc' for location, or sometimes they just have the name of the production company.

If on route you find yourself stuck in traffic and it looks like you are going to be late, make sure you call your emergency contact to let them know. If you think you will only be a few minutes late, you probably do not need to call, as the Assistant Director will be busy signing people in and probably will not notice you're missing. However, if you think you will be any more than ten minutes late, it is essential to let your contact know of your progress.

## YOUR CALL TIME

Having picked up your call time the night before, you should aim to arrive on set at least fifteen minutes early. If you are working first thing in the morning and the production company is providing breakfast, they may expect you to arrive earlier than your call time, for example 6.30am for breakfast before a 7am call. If this is the case, your agent should tell you when you pick up your details.

## ARRIVAL

Firstly, find your contact and let them know you have arrived. They will normally issue you with your salary voucher (or 'chit') for the day. You will be asked to fill in your name, address, contact number and National Insurance number. It is better to do this at the beginning of the day, so that if you misplace the voucher it can be returned to you. Keep the voucher with you all day — without it you will not be paid! On some jobs you may not get a voucher (particularly commercials, pop videos or photo shoots), and in these cases you will just be asked to sign a release form. The production company will then let your agent know the hours that you have worked. If you don't have a voucher, it's a good idea to make your own note of the time you were called, and the time you were wrapped (in other words told you were finished for the day, as in "that's a wrap!"), in case there's a discrepancy later.

Next, you will be asked to do one of four things. Depending on the call time, you may have breakfast. You may be sent into hair and make-up, or wardrobe. Lastly, you may be sent into the holding area or 'green room'. This is an area where the Assistant Director can keep everyone together, ready for the next instruction. Before reaching the holding area, you will normally go through hair, make-up and wardrobe.

## HAIR, MAKE-UP AND WARDROBE

Depending on what the production is, you may need to have your appearance changed in hair, make-up and wardrobe before you proceed to the set. The amount of time you spend in these departments partly depends on how well your agent has done their job, and partly on the type of production it is. Clearly, if you are working on a period production, the correct wardrobe is essential. However, present-day productions may require a costume also. If you are on a big call, these departments can be hectic, with dozens of people all being dressed at the same time. If you have a complex costume and you are not sure how to put it on, ask for help. Sometimes you may need to be seen by hair and make-up before you get into your costume, sometimes it is the other way around. The normal system is for your costume to have a unique number. Don't be too precious about being called by your number here — remember the crew are dealing with large numbers of people under huge time pressures and even if they wanted to call you by name, it would be impossible to remember them all. Your own belongings will then be given the same number and hung up in the wardrobe department, ready for you to collect at the end of the day. Do not leave large amounts of money or anything valuable with your belongings.

After wardrobe you may have to wait a long time before hair and make-up get to you. Once they do reach you though, they'll often only take five minutes, depending on what attention you need. There are exceptions — make-up may have a scar or wound to put onto you. This can take a long time, and be prepared to jump out of your skin when you look at yourself in the mirror afterwards! Women, on period productions particularly, spend longer being seen by hair. You may have already been for a haircut before the filming day. If not, they may want to trim your hair now. If you do have your hair cut, make sure you get the hairdresser to mark this down on your voucher, as it may mean you are entitled to an additional payment.

If you are given any prosthetics such as a beard or sideburns, or props such as a gun or sword, this will be marked on your voucher so that the production knows what to take back from everyone at the end of the day. If filming on location, you may not go into hair and make-up but they may come to you, and see to you in the holding area. Throughout the day on set you may have members of hair, make-up and wardrobe checking your appearance to make sure you still look exactly as was intended.

For many SAs, getting into an elaborate costume can be what makes a shoot worthwhile. Certainly, it's period and fantasy productions that SAs often find the most memorable. Here are a few experiences, both good and not so good...

*Band of Brothers* was the first production I ever worked on. I spent a week and a half as a POW, dressed in ragged clothes. I was made to look even thinner than I was by some make-up artists, and even got paid an extra £50 to have my hair shaved off. There were about 100 of us in total. We all got shuffled down to the set, which was a very impressive wooden and barbed wire holding centre, with 'dead' bodies all over the place, smoke, and crew running around trying to organise things. It was all very hectic, and I couldn't help but stand there and stare at what was going on... for the whole one and a half weeks, in fact!

**Daniel Baggs**

---

The most intriguing set I've ever been on was Ridley Scott's *Gladiator*, in early 1999. Anyone who is familiar with this Director's work will realise that to be an Extra on a Ridley Scott film is a real treat for anyone with an interest in design! Upon arrival at Bourne Wood, my first encounter was with the huge tents that had been set up to provide accommodation for all the soldiers' costumes for the battle sequences. After a quick change into my somewhat heavy outfit, I was transformed from 21st century man into a fierce Roman soldier. But here was the delight — the attention to detail was amazing! I was given muddy boots, real fur to wear on my legs and arms, and a fantastic array of fighting equipment which included a dagger worn around the waist, a metal spear and silver-grey armour breast plates (made from plastic), fitting snugly to the chest and shoulders. These were designed to give full articulation to the upper arm and shoulder area, and reminded me of an armadillo's natural armoured protection.

Complementing the weaponry was a typical Roman-style helmet designed to protect the neck, and also take away the last traces of the individual... it worked perfectly. Finally, a really hefty embossed shield made of fibreglass with a handle on the back was given to each and every soldier to carry. The set itself was an open forest, specially cut and cleared to accommodate the filming of *Gladiator*, with tall spindly trees flanking two hills disappearing into a small valley. I was required to visit this location several times, and each day was worth the journey just to feel the tremendous buzz and excitement from all involved. It was a wonderful team effort from everyone.

**Jeremy C. A. Goad**

---

There is a reason that corsets went out of fashion. It is called severe organ damage. It seems ladies of the Victorian period were in the curious position of being born without internal organs. They capitalised on this by accentuating their tiny waists and compressing their hollow torsos in fearsome articles of clothing made of stainless steel girders and coiled springs. Or maybe it was whalebone.

These days, in an effort to create as realistic a representation of the past as possible, Costume Designers have ingeniously recreated these instruments of torture, without taking into account the physiology of the modern woman. If you are lucky you may, like me, get to wear one in a period production.

There is no comfortable way to wear a corset. There is no comfortable position to sit in, and, above all, there is no technique yet invented (apart from the catheter) for going to the toilet whilst wearing a corset. The trick is not to drink. Or eat. This is fine, because the Costume Designer has taken for granted that you, the consummate method actor, have had your stomach and bladder removed. You will not feel like eating or drinking, as you will be too busy trying to avoid passing out.

Of course, I exaggerate: you might be able to manage a little food, such as a grape or two, and certainly a few sips of water. Plus, you will look *fantastic*. In a corset your posture is automatically improved, and you are given a new, elegant shape that you never knew you could have. It's just a shame that all that will be visible in the finished film is the back of your head.

**Bella Sabbagh**

## THE ZEN APPROACH TO WAITING AROUND

After navigating the wardrobe, make-up and hair departments, don't expect to find yourself on set immediately. Depending on how things are going, you may be kept in the holding area for hours and hours. In a studio this may be a room, on location it is more likely to be a bus parked at the unit base. If things are not going smoothly it is not uncommon to be held there all day and never be used. Hours can pass with nothing happening at all. Some people seem to wind themselves up about this and get flustered about hanging around. Now is the time your suitability to work as an SA will be tested. Can you do nothing at all without starting to feel like a rat in a cage?

Practising the age-old art of good conversation will help you pass this time. Because background work is more about what you look like than what you do, you could find yourself chatting to all sorts: doctors or old army generals, or perhaps even people who have served Her Majesty in more confined ways. Holding areas can be very sociable, and you will probably meet the kind of people you would not normally come into contact with. However, it can also be bordering on painful if you get stuck with someone who is intent on boring you to death. You can prepare yourself for this by making sure you have a good book and finding a quiet corner. The first conversation with anyone is nearly always about what you have worked on and what you're hoping to work on, and which agents are good and which are not. By the end of the day you will know of every production currently filming, and everything coming up. Suddenly, just when you've started to relax into the idea of not doing anything, you will be called onto a very busy set, and the pace of the day will pick up somewhat! Before we get on to that though, here are some more tips on the art of waiting around, plus one SA's advice on dealing with your colleagues:

You meet an awful lot of people in this business. A large proportion of them are on some sort of ego trip, with their mobiles on the go all the time. You often overhear conversations that sound like this: "Oh hello – yes I can do *Harry Potter* Thursday and Friday – no, I'm on the Bond film all next week. I'm available for *EastEnders* on the 18th – no, I'm casting for a McDonalds ad the next day. After that I'm on *Casualty* for three days." Makes you wish they were *in* casualty, not *on* it.

Do not pay too much attention to these people. The person who sits quietly in a corner reading their book is likely to be the most interesting. I once struck up a conversation with a woman in her late fifties, and after much prompting, she gradually told me about her life in the business. It transpired that she had been a stuntwoman in the 1950s and 60s. She had appeared many times in the hugely popular *Robin Hood* series of that time, and went on to work in the early Bond films, suspended on the end of ropes, dangling from double-winged aircraft in *Goldfinger*'s Pussy Galore sequence, and many other daring escapades. So, don't take too much notice of the mouthy ones in the green room. They have probably only had one day's work in the past six weeks!

**Ken Farmer**

Never take a train journey without any, or all, of the following: a Walkman, magazines, a good book and a bottle of mineral water.

These are vital, since you're almost guaranteed to get delayed, and hanging around with nothing to do draws out every single second. Playing I-Spy with the two trees and a cow outside your window will get boring very quickly.

The same applies to being a Supporting Artiste on a film set. There are few things worse than being sat in a marquee in the middle of the countryside with nothing to read or listen to while rain belts down outside, screwing up the Director's chances of getting the shot he wants. The other way to occupy yourself is star-spotting. It's fascinating to see how the 'talent' act when there's not a camera aimed at them. For example, Robert Redford (on *Spy Game*) prowled the set, hands in his pockets, giving out a glare that said, "Do not, under any circumstances, come near me unless your name is Tony Scott." Vinnie Jones signed a couple of autographs for Extras while frowning his way through *The Mean Machine*. Kenneth Branagh was polite, actually acknowledging the Supporting Artistes with a hello on the set of *Shackleton*. And while filming *28 Days Later*, Brendan Gleeson even tried to keep morale up on a cold Sunday morning by making me laugh a couple of times!

**James Lowe**

---

Waiting around: tune out or turn on? The options are as varied as the individual. Some activities, of course, tend to be frowned upon. Bagpipes are especially unpopular, as is Morris-dancing (unless essential to the plot) and any activity which intrudes into the exclusion zone around the 2nd AD. But a long shoot, punctuated by a moment or two of actual filming, can be put to any number of cerebral uses. Studying, catching up on correspondence, reading that book you've been meaning to read for ever, or working on the fifteenth draft of your script that "makes-this-piece-of-crap-look-like-amateur-night-and-someone's-actually-being-paid-for-it-there's-no-justice." Some people don their seven-league boots to walk off their lunch, some meditate, someone else sits fumble-fingered with a mandolin, a group of hardened 'lifers' argue over the good old days of Central Casting, some sneak a moment to hold hands under the cover of on-set action, and someone in the corner appears to be running an international conglomerate via their mobile phone. Time is a luxury, so use it. And you're being handsomely paid for it, too.

**Colin Giffin**

My advice is, take a novel. Not to read, to *write*. Believe me, you'll have time. I know one guy who's been writing a book for five years. Every time you see him on a set he's writing the same novel. It's probably about as long as the Koran by now.

**John Random**

## THE SET

By the time you've actually made it onto the set, you'll find that much of the mystique has already been removed by the waiting around, but it is still very important to be on your toes. Find your bearings and try to work out who everyone is. All members of the crew are usually in radio contact with each other, so a walkie-talkie is a good indication of someone being of importance. On bigger calls you could be faced with fifty or so crew members.

## WHO'S WHO?

Working as an SA, you are a small cog in a huge machine. To understand just how big this machine can be, have a read through this directory of who's who within the crew. All productions are split into three different stages of production: pre-production, shooting and post-production. During the shooting stage when you work as an SA, you will not come into immediate contact with all of the departments, but an understanding of the whole process will help make your day a little easier to comprehend.

A simple way to understand the hierarchy is to break down departments within a pyramid structure:

**Director**
**Producer, Writer**
**Camera, Lights, Sound, Editing, Music**
**Script, Casting, Stunts, Art Department**
**Wardrobe, Hair and Make-up, Props, Special FX, Visual FX**
**Transport, Locations, Construction, Catering, Accounts, Publicity**

This pyramid is bonded together by the production office and the

Assistant Directors, who liaise between the different departments.

## THE DIRECTORS

**The Director:** You will be surprised to see that the Director often isn't the person looking through the camera. They will probably be looking at the action on a monitor. The Director is the boss as far as creative decisions being taken and, mostly, what the Director wants, the Director gets. I was once told there are two rules to working on a film set: rule one, the Director is always right; rule two, refer to rule one.

**1st Assistant Director:** You may mistake him/her for the Director, since they are normally the person doing all the shouting and giving everyone their cues. They are the person in charge when you are on set. Make sure you listen very carefully to what they say.

**2nd Assistant Director:** Normally your first point of contact, but not always on the set as they are often at the unit base, planning ahead. The 2nd AD has the responsibility of making sure all members of the cast and crew are in the right place at the right time. This is the person who liaises with the agency about background requirements.

**3rd Assistant Director:** When you are on set, the 3rd AD is the person who will be looking after you. He/she liaises with the 1st AD and will be the person giving you instructions on where you should go.

**Production Assistants or Runners:** Literally as it sounds. They can be instructed do anything at all to support the ADs and the rest of the crew. This could be everything from moving people to and from the set, to taking lunch orders or picking up faxes.

As far as SAs are concerned, the Assistant Directors are your guides through the maze of film-making. They produce a daily 'call sheet' which details the order of filming — showing the scene numbers or parts of scenes that will be shot on that day — as well as an advanced schedule of what will (they hope) be filmed over the next few days. These are normally distributed in the evening for the following day. As an SA you will not automatically be given a call sheet, since they are only distributed amongst the crew. If you're lucky you may get a peek at one left lying around, or a friendly crew member may let you have a look if you ask politely.

On bigger productions the AD's department will be increased with a second 2nd Assistant or a Crowd Assistant Director, and lots of Runners.

## THE SECOND UNIT

Some productions may also have a Second Unit. This is a completely separate set of crew, normally reduced in numbers, but with its own Director and ADs. The second unit will complete scenes or parts of scenes that the main unit didn't have time for, or wants to re-shoot.

## THE PRODUCERS

**Executive Producer:** Usually the person who has put up the money for the production, or at least has built the partnerships to help finance the production.

**Producer:** Works with the Director, the financial backers and the Production Manager to ensure the production stays within budget. Ultimately they are also responsible for everyone on set. Some Producers can be directly involved with the Director in hiring the Scriptwriter, casting the actors or even selecting the Composer.

**Line Producer:** Not involved in the creative process, but may act as a go-between for the Producers and the Production Manager.

## THE PRODUCTION OFFICE

The Production Manager or Line Producer heads the production office. On bigger productions there may be several Production Co-ordinators that report to the Production Manager, and Production Assistants (PAs) that report to the Co-ordinators. The Production Manager takes care of things behind the scenes and delegates the responsibility of logistics on the set to the Assistant Directors.

## THE WRITER

Occasionally the same person as the Director, but not often. They work with the Director and his team to try to get their interpretation of the story made. Sometimes they are present on the set.

## THE CAMERA DEPARTMENT

**Director of Photography (DOP or Cinematographer):** Works with the Director supervising the camera and lighting departments to set up the shot. They are responsible for determining the look of the film in terms of style, rather than just the process of recording it.

**Camera Operator:** Works with the DOP and Director. They are responsible for operating the camera.

**First Camera Assistant (or Focus Puller):** In charge of setting up the right lenses and filters used on the camera. This is the person who 'checks the gate' after each shot.

**Second Camera Assistant (or Loader):** Responsible for loading and unloading the film in the camera, keeping all equipment clean and in good working order and generally helping the First Camera Assistant. This is the person who prepares the camera slate (or clapperboard) for each take.

**Grips:** This department works with the DOP and lighting department to help make the shot possible. This may involve building platforms, laying camera tracks for moving shots (and then pushing the camera during filming) or helping with blacking out for night shoots.

## LIGHTING

**Gaffer:** The team leader of the electricians who works with the DOP in setting out lighting plans in a safe way.

**Gaffer's Best Boy:** Like the First Camera Assistant, this is the first assistant electrician, assisting the Gaffer.

**Electricians (or Sparks):** Assist the Gaffer in all rigging of equipment.

**Generator Operator:** Maintains and operates the generators which are often needed to supply power in remote locations.

## SOUND DEPARTMENT

**Sound Mixer:** Responsible for operating all sound equipment. They monitor the quality of the sound as it is recorded and if more than one microphone is being used, they are responsible for mixing the sound at the appropriate levels.

**Boom Operator:** Working for the Sound Mixer, they are responsible for making sure the microphone is in the best possible place for sound recording. This may mean holding a boom above the action to get the microphone in closer. They also have to make sure that this boom never gets into shot.

## EDITING DEPARTMENT AND POST-PRODUCTION

**Editor:** Essentially they piece everything together in the editing room, working with the Director to help the development of the story with the footage that has been shot.

**Assistant Editors:** Usually one or two in number, they assist and report to the Editor.

**Dialogue Editor:** Works in post-production, to enhance the dialogue, getting the actors to re-record lines where necessary.

**Sound Effects Editor:** Has the job of adding in additional effects to give realism, such as a clock ticking or a door creaking.

## MUSIC

**Composer:** Works with the Director to give the film its mood by adding dramatic or emotive music. Not usually added until the film has been roughly edited.

**Music Editor:** The Composer will work with a Music Editor to make the composed music fit the required scenes.

## SCRIPT

**'Script Doctor':** Some productions may have 'Script Doctors', writers brought in to improve particular scenes, often at short notice, and sometimes during shooting. While this can be the original writer or writers, very often it isn't.

**Script Supervisor:** Responsible for taking detailed notes of each scene shot, particularly for continuity. They also record any dialogue changes and the length of each shot.

## CASTING

This stage is dealt with in pre-production, so it is unlikely that you will have any immediate contact with these people. The exception to this may be if you are auditioned for a Walk-on or small featured part.

**Casting Director:** Works with the Director, Producers and ideally the Writer, shortlisting actors who they think are suitable for consideration. The casting process is important to a film's success, in that one miscast actor can ruin the whole production. For this reason, casting of principal actors can sometimes take months in pre-production. The Casting Director has a good knowledge of all acting agents and their actors.

**Casting Assistant:** On bigger productions, a Casting Director may have an assistant to help with the casting of the smaller roles.

## STUNTS

**Stunt Co-ordinator:** Not always needed in every film, they are responsible for making sure that any stunt is carried out safely.

**Stunt Performer:** Where dangerous stunts are needed, each one of the actors will have a stunt double to take the plunge on their behalf.

## ART DEPARTMENT

**Production Designer:** Works with the Director and the DOP to complete the overall look of the production. They will co-ordinate set design and colour schemes within the whole production and work closely with the construction, wardrobe and props departments, to make sure everything looks as was intended.

**Art Director:** The person responsible for designing the sets that the Production Designer has come up with.

**Set Designer:** Works with the Production Designer and Art Director to produce models of each set that are then used to build the real sets.

**Storyboard Artists/Illustrators:** Help the Director create illustrations of key scenes (especially action sequences), shot by shot. Illustrators also work with the Art Director to show the DOP and Director how they intend a set to look.

**Set Decorator:** As it sounds, sets up the contents of the set: furniture, paintings, etc.

**Production Buyer:** In charge of buying materials and objects that may be used within set dressing.

## WARDROBE DEPARTMENT

**Costume Designer:** The team leader of the wardrobe department. They are responsible for the design and purchase of all costumes. They will liaise with the Director and the Production Designer to help give the production the right look.

**Wardrobe Supervisor:** In charge of the day-to-day running of the wardrobe department; overseeing costume fittings and making sure costumes are kept in good condition and not lost.

**Wardrobe Assistants:** On bigger productions the wardrobe department could have many other assistants to help with the day-to-day tasks of cleaning, fitting and maintaining costumes.

## HAIR AND MAKE-UP DEPARTMENT

**Key Make-up Artist:** A similar job to the Costume Designer, this person is the team leader of the make-up department, and has overall responsibility for the designing and applying of make-up. They will normally apply make-up to the leading actors.

**Assistant Make-up Artists:** Report to the Key Make-up Artist. They are the people who will come around the set making sure everyone's make-up is how it should be. Bigger productions may have lots of make-up artists.

**Prosthetic Make-up and Body Make-up:** Depending on need, a production may have a make-up artist applying specialist make-up.

**Key Hairdresser:** Supervises all the hairdressers who look after the SAs' hair. The Key Hairdresser will usually look after the actors' hair themselves, while the assistants help the SAs.

## PROPS

**Props Master:** Slightly different to the set dressers, they are in charge of specific props referred to in the script. This could be a sword, a photograph or any object that interacts with the main action.

**Prop Maker:** Responsible for making any specific props.

**Armourer:** On productions that involve weapons there may be a separate armoury department.

## SPECIAL EFFECTS (SFX)

**SFX Supervisor:** Responsible for executing safely all special effects, such as fire, wind, rain or snow. Often they will work with the Stunt Co-ordinator.

**SFX Technicians:** The SFX Supervisor will have a team of technicians that works to create any necessary effects.

**SFX Prosthetics:** Some productions may require parts of bodies to be blown off, or particular make-up effects.

## VISUAL EFFECTS (VFX)

On bigger productions this can be a completely separate unit of crew, with its own Director, Art Director and technicians. Otherwise it may just be a part of the art department.

**Visual Effects Supervisor:** The group leader of the visual effects department. VFX can range from working miniature models used in shot to computer generated imagery (CGI) added in post-production.

**Visual Effects Technicians:** Big fantasy or futuristic productions can have large numbers of VFX technicians, who often spend months in pre-production experimenting to get the desired effect.

## TRANSPORT

**Transport Captain:** Responsible for all drivers and vehicles, and getting members of the cast and crew to and from the set.

**Drivers:** The Drivers act as chauffeurs to key members of the cast and crew. They also act as couriers, moving things, vehicles and people from one location to another.

## LOCATIONS

**Locations Manager:** Not all scenes are filmed on sets. The Locations Manager is responsible for scouting suitable locations and securing their use for filming.

**Locations Assistants:** Report to the Locations Manager when sorting out logistical problems with locations, and work with local councils, the police and other services when dealing with the paperwork to secure locations for filming.

## CONSTRUCTION

**Construction Manager:** Works closely with the art department and is the leader of the team of builders who create the sets.

**Carpenters (or Chippies):** Since many sets are built out of wooden structures, they are an important part of the set-building process. Other construction jobs can include painters, plasterers, welders and drapery.

## CATERING

**Catering Supervisor:** To the SAs and some members of the crew, this is simply the most important person of all! They are in charge of supplying all of the food and drink for the cast and crew, within the given budget.

**Catering Manager:** It is generally accepted by Producers that if you feed your cast and crew well, they will perform better. The Catering Manager is usually part of an outside supplier that provides its own chefs.

## ACCOUNTS DEPARTMENT

The accounts department is an important part of the production office.

**Production Manager:** One of the Production Manager's main responsibilities is to keep all departments within the available budget. They will usually work with a Line Producer to ensure this happens.

**Production Accountant:** Responsible for all the production's outgoings and for ensuring that everyone is paid correctly.

**Assistant Accountants:** Usually given specific areas to look after, one of which will be the payment of all SAs.

## PUBLICITY

**Unit Publicist:** In charge of any press visiting the set, but more importantly is answerable to the Producer in terms of releasing early information about the production or, more crucially, preventing it from being leaked.

**Stills Photographer:** Takes photos throughout the filming process, which may be used later for press and publicity.

## OTHER CREW MEMBERS

Most productions have to have a unit nurse on set in case anyone is hurt during filming. Depending on the production there may be other crew members to look after animals or plants. Where children are involved, there may also be an on-set tutor. If specialist action is required, there may be other technical consultants, such as military or historical advisors.

## THE FILMING PROCESS

So, you're in costume, your hair and make-up are done, you've been led onto the set, and you've got a vague idea what the many crew members running around you are doing. What's next? Your first instruction will be from one of the Assistant Directors. They will show you your starting position for the shot, normally called "first positions" (or sometimes "number ones"), and discuss with you any action they require you to perform during the take. This could be as simple as making conversation with someone else in the background, or it could be walking from one point to another. When you are given your first position it is very important to make a mental note of exactly where it is, as you will have to go back to this spot a number of times.

You will then start a rehearsal, a walk through of exactly what happens in the scene. This is done to help all members of the crew. The camera department will practice its movement, the boom operator will move with the action, and the actors will walk through their movement and dialogue. With so many things to get right, it is not unusual to do several rehearsals before everyone is ready to go for a take. If you feel unsure about what you are supposed to do, this is the time to ask questions — nobody will mind during the rehearsal, that's what they are for. If you end up doing something drastically wrong during a take, you will soon know about it, and at the very least be given some strong words of advice on where you went wrong!

When the Director and all departments are happy with the rehearsal, the next thing you will be told is to prepare for a take. Wardrobe and make-up will be instructed to do 'final checks' and then, if you are filming at a studio, a red light will flash to warn everyone, and a bell will be sounded. The first instruction you will hear is "stand by" and then quickly afterwards the term "rolling", or "turning", or "roll camera" shouted out by the 1st AD. This means that the camera has started. Silence is crucial at this stage.

When it comes to a take, it is fairly normal for your cue to begin before the main action. You will hear "background action". Now is the time to really focus and do exactly what you have been told. If you are not started before the main actors, your cue may be to start with them, on "action". And if your cue is later than the main "action" you may be looking for your cue from a wave of the hand or even a tap on the shoulder. Make sure you keep following your instructions until you hear the word "cut". In a studio you will hear the bell sound twice, to signify the camera has stopped rolling. During shooting, don't look directly into the camera. This sounds obvious, but the camera can 'draw you in' if you're not careful. It is not necessarily a problem to look in the general direction of the camera if you have been told to.

The next term you hear will be "check the gate". The camera team will examine the lens of the camera to make sure it has no obstructions on it, such as a hair or dirt. One hair on the lens would appear as a giant worm on the screen, and ruin the whole shot.

At this point you will probably be told that you are "going again", as it is likely that several takes of the same shot will be needed. You will now be told to go to "first positions", and return to your starting position, ready to go again. After the shot has been completed, the camera will be moved and the same action will be filmed from a different angle. You will hear the term "resetting"; this is the crew's instruction to prepare for the next camera set-up. It can take a while to reset the camera, so you may be allowed to leave the immediate area, but do not go too far, as you can be called back suddenly. Usually a space will be provided on set for you to relax, normally around the refreshments.

## TERMS YOU WILL HEAR ON SET

**First positions:** Your starting point in the shot.

**Rehearsal:** A walk through of the take.

**Final checks:** Hair and make-up's last chance to get everything right.

**Red light and bell:** In the studio a red light will flash and a bell will be sounded when filming is about to happen. You may also hear "hold the red", meaning another take is about to happen, or "save the red", marked by two bells, meaning filming has stopped.

**Stand by:** Time to get ready.

**Rolling/turn over:** The camera has started.

**Background action:** Your cue to start.

**Action:** The principals' cue to start.

**Cut:** Stop the camera.

**Check the gate:** Making sure the camera lens is clear.

**Reset:** Moving the camera to a different position.

**Moving on:** A scene has been completed.

There are several other instructions you need to understand that may come up on set. The term "eye line" is more often used on the main actors, but if you are told what your eye line is, it simply means the direction you are required to look in.

You may be told that a scene is "miming only". Obviously the camera needs the appearance of a real conversation or speech, but the sound department can sometimes find it hard to concentrate on the principals' dialogue if there is a lot of background noise. Miming is the experienced SA's art form, and it can be harder than you think. This is where you may have heard of SAs silently repeating "rhubarb rhubarb rhubarb". It is probably a good idea to be a bit more natural than that, but don't panic, if you get stuck you could always recite a poem or song lyrics to yourself. Similarly, if there are a lot of people in the scene, shoe noise may sometimes be a problem for the sound department. Don't be surprised if you are asked to do a scene without any shoes!

You may be told that the sound department need to record a "wild track". This is to give a scene atmosphere and will be added in later during the editing process. Productions sometimes go to great lengths to get the right kind of wild track. The *Herald Sun* newspaper in Australia reported that when Peter Jackson, the Director of the *Lord of the Rings* trilogy, needed to simulate the noise of thousands of soldiers, he recorded the crowd at a cricket international. In the interval of a one-day match between England and New Zealand, Mr Jackson walked out into the centre of the pitch in bare feet and shorts, and gave instructions to the spectators on being in the battle of Helm's Deep for the second movie, *The Two Towers*. The stadium was reported to shake as the 25,000-strong crowd got into character. The local cricket fans were doubly pleased because as well as their brush with movie fame, New Zealand went on to beat England.

Working in a big crowd scene is something that all SAs will end up doing, probably sooner rather than later. Here's some first-hand advice:

Working as part of a big crowd is not much fun — unless you're sitting down all day and can hide a book under your costume. More often than not, you will be on your feet for long periods of time, usually somewhere outdoors (therefore cold), and you will not have a *clue* what is going on.

Remember that Hollywood cliché of the Director shouting orders down a big bullhorn? Well, no one carries those things, at least, not as often as they should. Consequently, orders issued to a large crowd of people in an exterior setting will get as far as the third row back (if you're lucky) and then be transmuted, via a kind of Chinese whispers process, another two rows, then peter out. If you're further than five people deep, you'd better be able to read lips.

Whether or not you hear the word "action" (assuming you know what your appointed action is) is not half so important as hearing the word "cut". If you are wearing a crippling pair of shoes and a seasonally inappropriate outfit on a street that's acting as a wind tunnel for the entire East End of London, the chances are that you will not wish to take one more step along the pavement than is strictly necessary. Hence the importance of "cut". Watching other people is not always advisable. Their chosen action might be to stop in the middle of the street during a take, and you don't want to cause a pile-up by getting the wrong end of the stick and hurrying back to your first position prematurely. Unfortunately, the only realistic solution is to carry on regardless until there is no room for doubt. When the 3rd AD scurries over and forcibly restrains you from moving any more, then you may assume the take is complete.

**Bella Sabbagh**

Scenes are not always shot in the order they appear in the script. If there is more than one shot with the same camera set-up, they will be shot consecutively. This saves time by avoiding unnecessary movement of the camera and crew. Here's a rundown of the main types of shots that you will encounter on set:

## THE MAIN TYPES OF SHOTS

**Close-up:** Of a person, the camera would be concentrating only on their head.

**Crane shot:** The camera may pan while up at a great height. A crane is used to lift the camera into the air.

**Establisher:** A general view of any location or building.

**Insert:** Close-ups of particular importance, such as a hand picking up a gun.

**Long shot:** Covers the whole height of a person with some of the background.

**Master shot:** Covers the main action all the way through with a wide shot.

**Mid shot:** Of a person, the camera would be concentrating only on the top half of their body.

**Pan:** The camera moves from left to right, or right to left.

**Pick-up:** Part of a scene to be re-shot.

**Reverse shot:** A 180 degree angle from the last position of the camera.

**Steadicam shot:** The camera is attached to a special counter-balanced harness worn by the camera operator. This reduces or eliminates the unsteadiness of the operator's motion.

**Tilt:** The camera moves either up or down.

**Tracking shot or dolly:** The camera moves smoothly forwards or backwards by running on tracks.

## CAMERA RIGHT AND CAMERA LEFT

It's important not to get confused by these simple terms. They describe the view from the *camera's* point of view, so if you are told to move camera left and you are facing the camera, you would actually move to your right, and vice versa.

## A WORD ABOUT CONTINUITY

During the filming of any scene, the camera will be moved around and the action will be filmed from different angles. Make sure you pay particular attention to your actions and movements, and repeat them in each take. If you are not doing exactly the same thing each time, when the sequence is edited together errors will appear. You should make sure everything stays consistent. For example, imagine you are filming a scene sat in a café with a long drink. In between takes you finish the drink. When the scene is edited together, from one angle the glass would be full, and from another angle (shot after you'd finished the drink) it would be empty. Similarly, do not under any circumstances (unless specifically instructed to do so) rearrange your costume between takes.

If you are used in a sequence that films over more than one day but involves you being in the same scene, this can also cause continuity problems. Don't forget that the finished film will edit together shots in the same scene that were actually filmed on different days. If you are in the scene one minute and disappear in the next shot, this will obviously cause a huge problem. It is therefore vital that if you are booked for a continuity sequence, you are available to work on *all* the days. Once you've started, you have to finish! Also be aware that if you are supplying your own costume on a present-day production filming over several days, you will have to wear the same clothes each day.

## CATERING

The catering on set is nearly always excellent. You may be surprised by how much you eat, and looking around at waistlines you'll probably notice that some members of the crew have got a bit too used to set food! When you are 'broken' for lunch, it is normal to see members of the crew being fed before you. Do not push in front of them; be polite and wait your turn. The chances are, while you have been hanging around the crowd holding area all morning, they have been rushing around non-stop. When the camera is not rolling, any production is costing the Producers a lot of money, so the quicker the crew are fed, the quicker they can start filming again.

As a general rule, when you are filming at a studio, you will be expected to pay for your meals, in the on-site cafeteria. If you are filming on location, meals will usually be provided. If you are filming on location and meals are not provided, there will normally be an additional meal allowance added onto your wages. Throughout the day, drink refreshments will be provided. You'll find that the food will often be a big topic of conversation amongst the SAs on set, and lots of comparisons with other productions will be made. You might hear a few stories like these:

Being fed and watered can be the highlight of a long day, especially when 'not being used'. I personally, like many of my female Extra friends, love the idea of someone else shopping, cooking and washing up — it's as good as being taken out for a meal!

However, one of my most humiliating experiences was on a period production when we were given raffle tickets for food (lack of free choice is always an indication of the level of the budget for Supporting Artistes). After negotiating the usual hazardous and costume drama-unfriendly steps to the catering, I waved my breakfast ticket to the catering lady, and asked for scrambled egg and bacon on my permitted bread roll. I was frostily told that it was not permitted to mix vegetarian with meat in the same bread roll!

You have been warned!!

Sue Hallett

Most times on-set catering is wonderful, wherever the set is. I can recall two old fellows dishing up first class grub in a remote field in the Peak District, for example. Occasionally things go badly wrong when inexperienced caterers get the gig, and so it was on one film I worked on, which was shot in Liverpool. The food was consistently bad. So much so, the Extras were going out to little cafes and greasy spoons downtown, and spending their own money (an unheard of occurrence). One day, the caterers had run out of the optional dishes and there was only a dreadful spaghetti bolognese left. Grumpily, the Supporting Artistes sat down on the catering bus to eat their meal. Suddenly, a young man leapt to his feet and began charging up and down the aisle waving something in his hand and screaming, "There's a f***in' teabag in me dinner! Look, a f***in' teabag!" He dived out of the bus, towards the catering van, where he was going to punch the chef's lights out. A nasty scene was narrowly averted by the intervention of the unit's security men. On the following day, a handwritten notice appeared on the catering van's menu board: 'We do not put teabags in our food, just bouquet garnis!'

**Ron Harrison**

---

Picture the scene: I'm working on *Gladiator*, and it is a bleak, frosty day in deepest rural Surrey. Hundreds of Roman soldiers are lined up behind defensive stakes. At the rear, catapults and scorpion crossbows are ready to unleash their projectiles of destruction on the Germanic barbarians camped in the surrounding woodland. There am I, resplendent in my Roman soldier's uniform, sword and spear at the ready, shield raised to fend off all comers. On the shout of "action!" I meticulously carry out my cue, only to be brought to a halt, rather too quickly, by the shout of "cut!"

A voice roars, "Where did those bloody Mars bars come from?" Where did they come from? Out of my armoured breastplate, that's where. Let this be a lesson to all potential Supporting Artistes: if you tend to get a bit peckish, don't stash supplies in your costume!

**Ambrose Pigott**

On film sets, certain clauses have been introduced to the rules to stop SAs being used for hours and hours without a meal break. If you're working under the FAA agreement, you will probably hear the term "broken lunch" (or sometimes "broken supper"). This clause is probably the single most argued about issue between ADs and SAs. It simply means that the production has to stop filming and break for a meal no later than five and a half hours from your call time, or from the end of the last meal break. If the production fails to do this, you are entitled to a broken lunch payment, which is the equivalent of one hour's overtime. There are specific exceptions to this. You may be asked up front to work a continuous working day; this means the production is allowed to keep shooting without a meal break, as long as a running buffet is provided. Please also remember that the broken lunch payment is only valid on FAA jobs. If you're working on a non-FAA job, you should still be given a meal break, but there may not be a penalty payment if it is not within a certain time.

## STAR STRUCK

The film business is full of extremely fragile egos. Everything you've heard about Hollywood stars has an element of truth. However, when they are working on set, ninety-nine per cent of stars are just like you — professional, well-mannered people. Knowing how to behave around them is not difficult. All that's required is that you treat them with respect. If you do end up in close proximity, behave naturally. Do not get star struck, do not ask for autographs and definitely don't start offering advice on how you think they should approach the scene!

On the other hand, if a principal does speak to you, do not ignore him or her either. The golden rule of being polite and friendly at all times to everyone is just as relevant when it comes to the leads. But do not speak to the Director or any of the actors unless they speak to you first. That said, it's important to recognise who they are. I once approached an artiste who seemed to be wandering around off set, and gave him a good telling off for not being in the holding area. It turned out to be Billy Zane, who was starring in the production being filmed on the stage next door. The point being that, despite my blunder, he was polite and calmly suggested I had probably mistaken him for someone else.

Here's a classic example of how *not* to behave around a star:

For the purposes of the film *Yentl*, the Mersey became the Hudson River, and one of the local ferries became a boat bringing émigrés from Russia to the New World. The boat was packed with hundreds of Extras, costumed as both rich and poor travellers. Barbra Streisand, who had written, produced and was both directing and starring in the film, had set aside this day for the big production number 'Poppa, Can You Hear Me?' The scene was to be done in one take, with multiple cameras. The Extras crowded the upper deck, staring expectantly, as directed, at the bridge. The great diva appeared, and the backing tapes rolled. There was a stunned silence as the song concluded; everyone was awed by the beauty of the moment. Finally, a little Liverpool woman stepped out of the crowd and said, "Why don't you sing us something we know, Barbra?"

On another day, Streisand was sitting alone in her Director's chair, deliberately isolating herself from the mass of Extras. A ten year-old girl had been trying to catch her eye for some time, and finally plucked up the courage to approach the big star. "How do you get to be an actress, Barbra?" she asked. The great one thought for a moment, and then gave a long and considered answer along the lines of amateur dramatics... drama school... repertory and touring companies... lots of luck... and concluded with the question to the little one, "Why do you ask?" "Oh well," replied the child, "I really want to be a nurse, but I haven't got the brains, so I thought I'd be an actress instead!"

**Ron Harrison**

## WHAT IF SOMETHING GOES WRONG?

When you are moving around any set, you should always have your wits about you. Watch out for cables you may trip on, or low-hanging props you could walk into. You don't need to worry about insurance too much. You will always be covered by the production company's insurance policy. Every set has to follow very strict health and safety regulations, with risk assessments completed before filming takes place. However, occasionally things won't go according to plan, and it is even possible that you might get hurt. Accidents are rare, but it is worth being aware that things can go wrong.

If you do get hurt, it is very important that you ask to see the unit nurse and report your injury, however insignificant. If your injury becomes worse after the event and you consider compensation, you will not have a case if the event was not reported when it happened. One of the benefits of union membership is that if anything does happen to you, they will be able to support your claim. For an additional annual fee, unions can arrange personal liability insurance.

As I've said, accidents are rare — but there are of course plenty of other things that can go wrong on a set, as the following stories show only too well...

There are many things which can catch you out on set, but wearing spectacles and forgetting to remove them can be one of the most embarrassing. The problem is that they become part of the anatomy, and nothing is worse than to go for a take on a period drama only to realise halfway through that you can still see everything clearly through your stylish modern frames... More often than not, vigilant continuity personnel spot such transgressions but, be advised, it can still happen. Contact lenses are therefore a great idea.

Mobile phones are never allowed on a set. It can be an annoying enough noise in normal social situations, but nothing will upset a Director and the lead actors more than to have a carefully constructed take interrupted by the shrilling of a phone that somebody has failed to turn off.

Tattoos are also a potential problem, principally because they can so easily be dated. In the BBC Victorian drama *Murder Rooms: The Dark Beginnings of Sherlock Holmes*, I had to be a tattooed man in a circus. A condition of the part was that I had *no* actual tattoos, because they needed to appear authentically Victorian, and a great deal of research had been undertaken by the make-up department to ensure total accuracy. It is for this same reason that all personal jewellery must be removed (although wedding rings can, if necessary, be taped over), and the best time to remove them is before you leave for the shoot. You may think that a necklace or wristwatch won't be seen, but unnecessary retakes are expensive and it is always better to be safe than sorry.

**Malcolm Lauder**

---

I was working, along with hundreds of others, on *102 Dalmatians*, the successful Disney film. The location was Kings Cross railway station, and it was a night shoot. In fact it was the last day of shooting, and the unit was doing a series of pick-up shots and re-shoots. Time was very important, and limited from about 10pm to 5am, when the trains would start to roll again. The shots were varied and quite involved. The crew was on a strict schedule and had probably four or five scenes to shoot.

By 3.00am, we'd reached the penultimate shot, and everyone was becoming a little tired and listless, except the two excellent Dalmatian puppies who were starring in that scene. They were to be placed in a 'quarantined area', because they were not old enough to have had their inoculations. We SAs were to pass by them with a roving camera viewing us from a dogs'-eye view. After two rehearsals with dummy dogs, the dog handler and the real puppies were carried onto the set. In the meantime, the designated quarantine area of about 1.5 square metres was cordoned off with cones, and the area was sprayed and cleaned thoroughly with disinfectant, a painstaking job. Anyone who stepped into this area had to wear special shoes.

Another rehearsal followed. The real dogs stood still, the cones were removed and we all passed by closely, but careful not to step into the quarantine area. The time was now approaching 4am. We were all ready to go, but unfortunately we were due a tea break. The cones were replaced. The 1st AD told us how important it was that *nobody* stepped inside them. The guy had a bullhorn, so everyone must have heard, but unfortunately in the confusion and hurry to get a snack and a drink, two people ignored him, or forgot, or just did not listen to the instruction — and walked right through the cones.

All of a sudden, the air thickened and turned blue, as a crew member completely lost his cool, and proceeded to explain using a variety of expletives that it would take another half hour to set the quarantine up again, the first f***ing train was due in within the hour, and we still had another shot to do. He was *not* a happy man. The guilty SAs shuffled away into a corner. The crew did not get their break. Luckily the shot was a one-take success, and the last shot was hurried through in about half an hour, with us being wrapped at 5.15am.

It's funny looking back, but at the time it was a nightmare for the crew — all because someone did not listen.

Graham Frosdick

While filming *The Four Feathers* on location in Morocco, we were hit by one of many sandstorms, as usual completely unexpectedly. We promptly ran back to the unit base and while trying to get Ahmed to open his tea wagon, a call came over the radio that one of the Extras was missing, presumed still on set. I put on my face veil and headed back to the last position we were in, which was very difficult as visibility was down to a few feet. After having to scour the area almost with my fingertips, I found him huddled on the ground, making himself the warmest, tastiest morsel around for the local scorpion population. I got him back safe and sound, and to this day can only presume he was asleep, or completely stupid not to notice what was happening around him. It pays to keep your eyes open!

**Richard Manlove**

---

After waiting in the green room for eight hours on the final afternoon of a shoot set in a restaurant, I was relieved when the Director told me, "We just need to do some hand shots of you and we'll be wrapped." The Designer made a big song and dance of setting the slice of gateau on the plate at just the right angle, and fussed around presenting it attractively on the table. My role as a waitress was to dribble the cream tantalisingly around the cake.

"It's the last piece of cake," said the Designer, "so just pretend to pour it for the rehearsal and we'll have to do just one take." Having mimed it a few times, we were ready. On "action", I lifted the jug and tilted it slightly. The cream slid slowly towards the spout, teetered on the lip and then the entire contents fell out in one glutinous lump onto the gateau — the result of a whole day under the hot lights. I bet that Designer will keep some cream in the cool box next time!

**Stephanie Barrows**

## THE END OF THE DAY

You will know the filming day is over when you hear the magic word "wrap". This is not to say that you will necessarily be kept until the end of the day. It is normal for groups of SAs to be wrapped throughout the day, as soon as their filming is complete. This is important to the production, as releasing artistes early will obviously save them money. On big calls it can take up to a couple of hours from wrap before you are actually on your way home. The earlier process of arrival is reversed, and you may have to go back through hair and make-up, then back through props and wardrobe, before you come to the moment of truth — signing off.

Please remember that everyone is as keen to get home as you. A queue is never fun, but after a long day on set this is what you will be faced with. The crew are tired, you are tired, and tempers can become frayed. Your payment will need to be authorised by a member of the crew, usually an Assistant Director, before you can leave. They will add any additional payments you are entitled to, such as overtime, and then sign your voucher. They then ask you to sign it, before giving you a copy to take home with you.

If you think the details of your payment are incorrect, it is important to say so, since leaving it until later will inevitably mean the mistake will not be rectified. However, try to do this in a friendly, polite manner. Do not get into a shouting match about your payment. Claiming that the AD has not paid you what you are entitled to will not go down very well. If it looks like they are not going to budge, your best bet is to politely but firmly tell them that you do not agree with them, and before you sign the voucher write 'disputed' on it. When it is convenient, let your agent know what has happened and they will look into it for you.

Refusing to sign the voucher will not help you, and could indeed result in you not being paid anything at all. Be careful not to get caught up in the heat of the moment. You only have to look at a football match to see that crowds can behave in strange ways, and it has been known on sets for one or two SAs to whip a crowd up into a frenzy over a disputed payment that they are not entitled to anyway. If you have a problem, make sure you are 100 per cent confident that you are in the right before pursuing it.

You will not, I'm afraid, be leaving the set with a wad of notes in your pocket. You will receive your payment later, via your agency, who will first take their commission. For more details on how this works, and the various rates of pay you can expect, see Chapter 6.

# DIFFERENT TYPES OF WORK

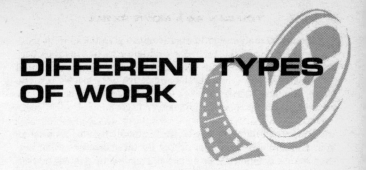

Working as a Supporting Artiste can encompass much more than just the movies and TV — you could be used in any medium that requires people. The other obvious avenues are commercials, pop videos, photographic jobs and the Internet. Less obvious are promotional work, publicity stunts, corporate or training videos and even police identity parades!

## TELEVISION

One of the great things about the expansion of television channels in recent years is the increase in the production of programmes. Digital and satellite TV does mean more repeats, but it also means more new TV dramas, soaps and sitcoms, which in turn leads to more work for SAs. Soaps often have regular SAs and, as noted earlier, some even become familiar faces to the audience, helping to create the sense of a real community. For the lucky few working on a soap, it can become a full-time job.

TV dramas can be one-offs, or be anything up to about twelve episodes in a series. Your agent will be wary about using you too often on multi-episode series, but if you're lucky you may be able to work on the same drama more than once, as long as the episodes are far enough apart to avoid you being remembered by viewers. Other types of TV work you could be asked to do include reconstructions (for documentaries or programmes like *Crimewatch*) and sketches for comedy programmes.

## IDENTS, PROGRAMME PUBLICITY AND TRAILERS

Station idents are those five-second clips you see between programmes that brand the station you are watching, and can sometimes make use of SAs. The audience's attention span is becoming shorter and shorter these days, and in an attempt to grab the viewers, more and more money is being poured into the adverts you see for particular programmes. These trailers typically use a twenty-second clip of the show in question, but the more creative ones involve separate filming. You may be asked to work on a trailer for a programme without ever actually being in the programme itself.

Sometimes on films, you may be used in publicity for that production. This could mean a photo shoot for the movie poster, or perhaps some extra filming for a special 'stand alone' trailer, or even additional footage for the DVD extras. Your association with a film could even go beyond publicity and into merchandising: some SAs, who have had featured roles or Walk-ons in the right kind of Hollywood blockbuster (such as the *Star Wars* films), have found themselves being turned into an action figure! Unfortunately, the release you sign on the day allows the production company to use your image in any way they want without paying you any additional money. A toy version of yourself makes a nice souvenir though!

## COMMERCIALS

Lots of types of work fall under the umbrella of commercials. You could be used as part of a billboard campaign, a TV advert or a magazine advert, or be used across all media in the same campaign. If a commercial is photographic, or requires little or no dialogue, Directors will often consider SAs as well as actors. For this reason commercials can be very lucrative, and if you get featured in a commercial the rewards can be high. However, just being in a commercial doesn't necessarily guarantee the big money — working in the background of a commercial is paid at similar rates to background work in TV and film. (See Chapter 6 for more details.) Here's one SA's experience of working on a major TV ad:

> Naturally, I'd felt the casting had gone horribly, and that I'd made a complete fool of myself, so surprise would be a mild way of describing my reaction to the news that I'd been chosen for a Walk-on in a BT advert. My timid hopes of actual screen time and a decent paycheque were eclipsed by the joy I felt when I was told that a car would be picking me up to take me to the location. This, to me, was the ultimate luxury. As a non-driver, I have a profound hate-hate relationship with all forms of public transport, and the

bliss (and novelty) of sitting back and letting someone else drive me across London was a real bonus.

The location was small and cosy... very cosy. The scene took place in somebody's one-bedroom flat — the kind described by estate agents as 'bijou'. The crew and equipment were all crammed in there, and had been all morning. The result was an assortment of interesting odours, and a lack of any discernibly fresh air. The cold takeaway on the table wasn't helping to improve the atmosphere much.

I spent several hours in the wardrobe and make-up trailer, being fitted with a pair of nasty trousers and a tight T-shirt, and painted with enough make-up to last me a week. Then I was called on set with the two other girls who were playing my fellow guests. The scene involved being greeted at the door of the tiny flat by the lead actress, and squeezing our way past her into the room. That was pretty much it, but, needless to say, we had to do it many, many times. In the next scene we were seated around a table, with the congealed takeaway on plates in front of us.

It was all so different from being pedestrian number 237, or standing on a freezing hillside wearing Y-fronts over my trousers (for Comic Relief... need I say more?). In addition to the ease of the job, the results were on TV within a matter of weeks, and for once, people I know were able to actually see my face on screen!

**Laura Tilly**

## POP VIDEOS

Pop videos, referred to in the business as 'promos', are the less glamorous relation of film and TV work. Normally organised at short notice and often filmed in a day, they generally involve very long hours, and can be fairly painful for the SA. The shoot may continue on and on (up to twenty hours has been known) without proper breaks, and does not always involve good catering. You may be offered the work for a flat fee for the day; it is always worth asking before you accept the job how long the day will be before you go into overtime. Because the British music industry is centred there, the majority of pop promos are made in the London area. The following SA's experience is from a two-day video shoot (suggesting a more expensive production than most), but it was still far from comfortable!

The setting was a 1970s party in a church hall, with the band playing on a small stage, and a bar at one end of the dance floor. The main impediment to my enjoyment of this, my first pop video experience, was the dress I was given to wear. I'd been to a casting, where I'd left my details, including dress size. I'd also had a follow-up call to ask for my details, including dress size.

The dress they gave me was a minimum of two sizes too small. It was pink, frilly and wafty, and once I had been crammed into it, I discovered a number of large gaps through which my underwear (and worse) could be clearly viewed. The one positive result of this was that I spent most of the two-day shoot sitting down instead of dancing, as my rear view was unsuitable for family audiences. I remained seated while the majority of the other Extras danced to the same song over and over and over and over... you get the picture. I watched from the relative comfort of a bench as the crew and bulky camera equipment moved through the crowded room with only a cursory notion of spatial awareness, which resulted in several near clashes of dancer and rigging.

For some reason, half the crowd consisted of Russians who spoke no English, so miming conversation during each take became a bewildering exercise in sign language and guesswork. The room became hotter and hotter as the day went on, and as the props drink I was holding was some watered down concoction that was currently with its fourth owner, and my dress (into which I had now been sewn) allowed for only the shallowest of breaths, I began to feel a little odd. It's just a mercy that I didn't have get up and dance, and that the sympathetic ADs had a plentiful supply of water. Fortunately, I have never heard the song or seen the video since its release. I don't think I could cope with the flashbacks.

**Bella Sabbagh**

It's worth mentioning here that casting-wise, commercials and pop videos work a little differently and perhaps a little less traditionally than other productions. Competitive Directors have become obsessed with the idea of using 'real' people. This is not to say that actors are not 'real' (although I'm sure some would suggest that by definition they are not). What Directors want are people who look 'fresher', who have not been seen on screen before. Secondly, these 'real' people will also probably have no preconceptions of what it means to be a performer and are therefore, in principle, far more malleable.

Since most Directors cut their teeth on commercials and pop promos, they form an excellent arena in which to be more adventurous. Because of the time scales involved (thirty seconds for a TV commercial, three minutes or so for a pop video) and with little or no dialogue, Directors are able to 'get away with' far more than in, for example, a ninety-minute movie. A cynic might suggest that they also get away with paying 'real' people less as well, but if you've got a good agent this will not happen. Often with these types of productions, a Casting Director will be appointed to do a street casting and literally pull suitable 'real people' off the street. As mentioned above though, the upside is that they will often consider SAs, as well as actors, for Walk-on parts.

## MODELLING

If you look right for a particular campaign, you could find yourself doing some modelling. Unless you are represented by a model agency, this is unlikely to be strutting the catwalk though. More likely is catalogue modelling, or modelling for a fashion shoot in a magazine. Style magazines occasionally look beyond the typical domain of the thin and beautiful — we have cast photo shoots with very old models as well as larger-than-life, bubbly characters. Unfortunately, for some SAs, things don't always end up going to plan...

I once had to go to a casting for a photo shoot in Manchester, for an Italian sports clothes company. This was going to be quite a prestigious colour spread in 'lads' magazines, but I had been told nothing about the actual modelling. The photographer loved me, continually remarking how Italianate I looked, and how right my hair was. Gradually I realised, as he reluctantly dribbled the words out, that I was supposed to be an Italian grandfather who had just died, and was surrounded by his children and grandchildren. This was to be the posed shot! He photographed me lying down; first with eyes open, then with them shut. The photographer's joy knew no bounds and I was already spending the considerable fee in my head, fired by his enthusiasm. Then he was finished, and assured me that I would be hearing from him, via my agent. As I was making my way through the door, he called me back and asked how broad I was. When I replied that I did not know, he put a tape measure across my shoulders. "Oh dear," he said, "I think there'll be a problem with the coffin." This was the first I'd heard of any coffin. He clucked disappointedly, and sadly shook his head. Yes, I lost the job. I was too fat for the coffin.

**Ron Harrison**

## OTHER PHOTOGRAPHIC JOBS

You could be asked to do Editorial work, appearing in photos specially taken by newspapers or magazines to illustrate articles. In advertising, photographers often need parts of people to give products naturalism; a photo of a cigar in close-up may look better in someone's hand for example. Some artistes specialise in hand modelling, or even foot modelling for shoes, and there are specialist agencies who deal exclusively with such people.

## WORLDWIDE WEB FAME

Today advertising agencies and marketing gurus include websites in their overall campaign. If you have been used in a photographic advert do not be surprised to see that part of your fee covers Internet usage.

## CORPORATE AND TRAINING VIDEOS

If you've ever been in a job where you had to watch a training video, you probably know how dull they can be. However, from the casting point of view, they can involve role-play acting, and big companies sometimes employ talented SAs as a less expensive alternative to using actors. Corporates can therefore be a really useful training ground for testing out and improving your acting ability — if you have any. But be aware, because the usage of training videos is restricted, daily fees are negotiated and can be lower than for film and TV jobs.

## PROMOTIONAL WORK AND PUBLICITY STUNTS

This can actually be more regular than film and TV work, but is not normally as well paid. Some Supporting Artistes take promotional jobs in between filming to supplement their income. You could be employed to look glamorous handing out leaflets on a stand in an exhibition, or giving out free samples in a supermarket. If you are particularly unlucky you may be dressed up as a giant coffee bean and put in the middle of Oxford Street (such things happen, believe me). Occasionally you could be booked for a 'crowd scene' that will not be filmed — large-scale publicity stunts sometimes involve hiring big crowds to attract attention in commuter areas such as train stations.

## I'M INNOCENT!

You may be asked to take part in a police line-up. Normally the police organise these themselves with their own street casting, approaching members of the public who have a similar appearance to the suspect, but increasingly police forces are handing this job over to the experts — the casting agencies. This is particularly true if the crime is very serious, or if the police find it difficult to get other people with a similar appearance. We were recently asked to cast a police line-up of drag queens!

It is possible that you will not even be used, as the suspect has the option of removing anyone from the line-up that he/she doesn't like the look of. The police therefore always have more people than they need, though obviously you will still be paid. The money for police line-ups is not particularly good, but they are usually very quick, one to two hours at the most. Some people are a bit paranoid about doing line-ups, but don't panic — if you are picked, it doesn't mean you get put in prison!

## BEING IN THE AUDIENCE — THE PRICE IS NOT RIGHT

Game shows and sitcoms often record in front of a live audience. You can normally get tickets for these free of charge by writing to the production company involved (or by looking out for ads in the paper inviting you to ring in for tickets), but you will not be paid to be in an audience. However, it can be an interesting way of watching the production process, particularly for those with no experience.

## WHEN WILL YOU SEE IT?

When you've done your day on set, a common question is, "When do I get to see the end result?" This depends on what type of job it was. A feature film can take over a year in the post-production stage before it finally hits the big screen. On the other hand, a commercial can literally be filmed one day and on TV the next. Supporting Artistes also often ask if they are going to be credited. The simple answer to this is no. On a film, credits are given at the Producers' discretion and it would simply take too long to list all the SAs individually. If you were very lucky, and had a Walk-on part that was referred to in the script, you could be credited, but this is not automatic (you will however usually be credited if you were an actor's Stand-in or double: see Chapter 7). You may be credited collectively in the form of your agency getting a mention. Television credits are normally dictated by the overall policy of that channel, and with a lot less screen time available than film, SA credits on TV productions are even less likely.

Getting hold of a copy of your work can be equally difficult. When you are on set, you could politely ask the crew where and when the production is going to be shown. Certainly with TV work, your best bet for getting a copy is to video it yourself. However, you might be working on a commercial that is only going to be shown abroad, or a photo campaign where the production company may not know which newspaper or magazine it will appear in. Your best chance in these cases is to find out which advertising agency you are working for, then ask your agent to get you a copy from them. If that doesn't work, you could always phone the advertising agency at a later date.

## IF YOU'RE NOT COMFORTABLE, SAY SO BEFORE IT'S TOO LATE

In your career as an SA you will be asked to a variety of jobs, involving all manner of ridiculous things (anyone who has seen Channel 4's bizarre betting game show *Banzai!*, which regularly uses SAs, will know quite how ridiculous I mean). You could be asked to do nudity, kiss someone, or even perform simulated sex. You could be asked to smoke, eat something unpleasant, or play a dead body. (But rest assured that anything dangerous, like fighting or driving at high speed, would be done by qualified Stunt Performers.) If you are asked to do something that you're not comfortable with, it is much better to say that when you're first offered the work by your agent. Arriving at a job and then refusing to do what you've been booked for will cause a big problem!

# GETTING PAID

While you're enjoying the novelty of your first few jobs, money may not be uppermost in your mind, but you'll soon realise that few people work as a Supporting Artiste just for the love of it. Before you accept any assignment, you need to understand how much you will get paid and what deductions will be made, as well as how long it will take for you to actually receive your wages.

With fees in the business constantly changing, it would be impossible to give exact illustrations here of what you will be paid for each different type of job you might do. The aim of this chapter is to arm you with a rough idea of the fee you can expect, in an attempt to prevent you from being ripped off. There are quite a few different payment agreements in operation, covering various types of work. As you'll see from the details later in this chapter, though some agreements are similar, they're not all identical. It's a good idea to familiarise yourself with them, to avoid confusion, especially with situations where you think you're due a fee which doesn't actually apply under the agreement you're working to (though it may apply under other agreements).

The details given below are not exhaustive, but should give you a good idea of how payment works, along with a working knowledge of each of the various payment agreements. These details were current when this book was written, in summer 2002. But please remember, this is only a guide — always check that the agreement you are working to hasn't changed or been updated since then.

## WHAT YOU PAY AN AGENT

Your casting agency, like you, will not work for free. The hundreds of phone calls, staff wages and other office overheads have to be paid for! Sometimes an agency will charge the production company direct-ly, by adding on an agency fee to any work offered to an artiste. However, this is not the norm, and in an extremely competitive mar-ket there are always agencies willing to waive any agency fee to get the work. This means the agency has to get its income from you — the artiste. This is normally done by your agent deducting a commission from any earnings you receive for work they've found you.

Commission rates vary from thirteen to twenty per cent, but the aver-age is about fifteen per cent. In addition, the commission will also have VAT added to it (at seventeen and a half per cent). Just as an example, let's say you earn £100 for a job. Your agency's commission rate is fifteen per cent, so that's £15. Seventeen and a half per cent of £15 is £2.62, so the commission deducted will be £17.62, leaving you with £82.38.

## REGISTRATION FEES

The DTI and the unions are working hard to stop agencies taking big up-front fees from SAs. This is because in recent years lots of busi-nesses have sprung up claiming to offer work, but only after you've paid a registration fee. This fee can vary between £25 and £250, and in some cases (as noted in Chapter 2) the agency disappears after it has taken your money.

You may be asked to pay a fee to have your photo and details put into a casting book (which is sometimes payable each time that book is updated). Ideally, you should not have to pay any agent any fee before they have found you work. The better agencies will deduct a one-off cost from your first job, or they may not charge you a fee at all. Certainly, if you are asked to pay any fee above £75 per year, you should think carefully about staying with that agency.

## GENERAL POINTS ABOUT WHAT YOU EARN

The money you will make is dependent on three important factors. Firstly, the medium the job is for, ie, film, TV or commercial. Secondly, how featured you are, ie, background, Walk-on or actor. Finally, the usage: is it going to be shown in one country or worldwide? If it's a commercial, will it be shown for a few months, a year or more?

The film and TV business is a seven-days-a-week, twenty-four-hours-a-day machine. Do not expect any additional payments for working on a Saturday or Sunday. However, some agreements do have a higher rate for night shoots, or working on a public holiday. All of the agreements include an unpaid meal break during the working day, normally an hour. It is important to be aware that you may not always be working to a particular pay agreement. Film and television productions have the most rigid pay structures. Other areas of work may just be for an agreed daily rate, with overtime, but no other additional payments. Always check with your agent what the payment will be before accepting a job.

## HOLIDAY PAY

Unlike full-time employees, working as an SA you do not receive normal paid holiday. However, following a ruling by the European Court of Justice in June 2001, under UK legislation freelance workers and those on short-term employment contracts *are* entitled to paid annual leave from the first day of their employment. If you are working to FAA or Equity agreements as a Walk-on or SA, an amount for 'untaken holiday' will be paid in addition to the daily fee. This is usually worked out at one twelfth of the daily rate (and has not been added to the examples of rates given below). Although an allowance for untaken holiday is now a legal right, it may be that if you are working under any other kind of contract, for a negotiated fee, the production company are assuming that your 'holiday pay' is included within that fee.

## FILM AND TELEVISION

In most cases when working on a film, the release form is a complete buyout of all of your rights. This means the film can be shown anywhere in the world in perpetuity, and you will not receive any additional payments. Make sure you know which agreement you are working to. Within a forty-mile radius of Charing Cross in London, the PACT/FAA Agreement is usually used. This agreement is also sometimes used for television productions. Outside of the forty-mile radius you may be working to the Equity/PACT Walk-on and Background Artist Agreement.

## THE PACT/FAA AGREEMENT

The PACT/FAA Agreement hasn't changed since 1997, apart from an additional daily payment for holiday pay that was agreed in October 2001. Day and night rates are for a nine-hour stipulated time period, after which you will go into overtime.

## WHAT YOU COULD EARN UNDER THE PACT/FAA AGREEMENT (LAST UPDATED 1ST FEBRUARY 1997)

|  | Standard Day | Standard Night | Shift Call |
|---|---|---|---|
|  | (7am-10pm) | (4.30pm-6.30am) | (4 hours) |
| Daily Rate | £64.50 | £80.62 | £40.31 |
| Hourly O/T | £12.09 | £15.10 | £6.05 (15 min) |

**Notes:**

Overtime on a standard day or night begins after eight working hours (that is, nine hours including one unpaid hour for a meal break). On a four-hour shift call, £6.05 is paid if filming runs over by up to fifteen minutes. If it's more than fifteen minutes, your pay is automatically upgraded to a standard day rate.

If you are called between 6am and 7am you will receive an additional £7.50 per half hour, until 7am.

A higher pay scale is used on public holidays.

Broken lunch (see Chapter 4 for details) starts five and a half hours from call time and the second broken meal occurs after twelve hours. Paid at £12.09.

If you are required to go to an audition, you receive £20 at a recognised studio and £10 anywhere else (payable whether or not you actually get a part).

The fee for attending a costume or other type of fitting is £20.

Under the FAA agreement, other additional payments are varied, and fall under two main categorie. Firstly, Supplementary Performance Fees (for firing a gun, swimming, dancing, driving, cycling, horse riding, 'special reaction' and dialogue) and secondly, Supplementary Service Fees (for bringing a car, cycle, dog, change of clothes or special clothing, having a haircut, being wetted down or doubling).

Travel allowance payments (distances measured from Charing Cross): Calls at a recognised studio: £5. Calls over ten miles and up to twenty miles: £5. Calls over twenty miles and up to forty miles: £8.50. Calls at or before 6am regardless of location: £8.50

Your agent is not allowed to take commission from the following payments: haircuts, supply of car/dog/cycle, costume allowances, auditions, fittings or meal allowances. (Note that this only applies under the PACT/FAA agreement, and not under other agreements.)

## THE EQUITY/PACT WALK-ON AND BACKGROUND ARTIST AGREEMENT

If you are working outside of the forty-mile radius on a film or TV production with an independent producer or production company, you may be working to the Equity/PACT Agreement (though it is true to say some productions, especially movies, filming outside the forty mile zone often choose to ignore this agreement, and negotiate their own, usually slightly lower rates). Under this agreement, SAs are known as Background Artists.

## WHAT YOU COULD EARN UNDER THE EQUITY/PACT AGREEMENT (LAST UPDATED 1ST APRIL 2002)

|  | Standard day | Standard Night |
|---|---|---|
| **Background Artist** |  |  |
| Basic Daily Rate | £64.10 | £96.15 |
| Overtime Per Half Hour | £5.34 | £8.00 |
|  |  |  |
| **Walk-ons** |  |  |
| Basic Daily Rate | £86 | £129 |
| Overtime Per Half Hour | £7.16 | £10.74 |
| Multi-Episodic Day Rate | £129 |  |

Definitions:
**Background Artist:** Appears in vision, but not required to give individual characterisation or speak dialogue, except that of crowd noises, which shall not be deemed to be dialogue in this context.

**Walk-on Artist:** Is required to exercise professional skills in relation to a cast actor or actress and/or in close-up to camera and be required to impersonate an identifiable individual and/or speak a few unimportant words where the precise words spoken do not have an effect on the overall script or outcome of the story.

**Notes:**
Overtime begins after ten hours. Hours of work are nine out of ten hours a day, with an hour for an unpaid meal break.

Walk-ons in TV productions could also receive repeat fees. This is 100 per cent of the daily rate per repeat transmission on UK terrestrial channels (that's BBC1, BBC2, ITV1, Channel 4 and Channel 5).

Costume fittings are paid at £36 for a full day, £19.50 for a half day.

Additional payments for special skills are various and are negotiated, subject to a minimum of £16.90.

When forty-one or more Background Artists are called on a day or night, the terms of this agreement shall not apply, and each Background Artist will receive an individually negotiated fee.

## OTHER EQUITY AGREEMENTS

In addition to the Equity/PACT Agreement, ITV, BBC and TAC (Welsh Independent Producers) have their own agreements with Equity. Here's a rundown of details:

### WHAT YOU COULD EARN UNDER THE BBC/EQUITY AGREEMENT (LAST UPDATED 1ST JULY 2001)

|  | Standard Day | Standard Night |
|---|---|---|
| **Supporting Artiste** | | |
| Basic Daily Rate | £73.60 | £80.50 |
| Hourly Overtime | £11.30 | £13.90 |
| | | |
| **Walk-ons** | | |
| Basic Daily Rate | £91 | £110 |
| Hourly Overtime | £13.90 | £18.50 |

**Definitions:**
**Supporting Artiste:** Is not required to give individual characterisation in a role or to speak dialogue beyond crowd noise or reaction.

**Walk-on Artist:** Is not required to give individual characterisation in a role but may be required to impersonate an identifiable individual, to accept individual direction and to speak a few unimportant unscripted words where the precise words spoken do not matter.

**Notes:**
Overtime begins after eight working hours. This works out to be a nine hour day, with one hour unpaid for a meal break. On location this becomes nine and a half hours if travel time is being paid.

Night work is work scheduled either to extend beyond midnight or to begin between 10pm and 7am. Day work which extends into unforeseen work after 12.15am will be paid at night overtime.

Walk-ons may also be entitled to repeat fees, though SAs are not.

If two or more programmes are recorded on a single day, a multi-episodic payment of an additional fifty per cent of the fee will be paid.

Other additional payments vary and can fall under seven categories: special skills, nudity and simulated sex, strenuous work, costume and make-up, provision of costume, length of hair, and auditions.


## WHAT YOU COULD EARN UNDER THE ITV/EQUITY AGREEMENT (LAST UPDATED 1ST APRIL 2002)

Perhaps the most clearly defined of the lot. Under this agreement SAs can be given three different grades: Walk-on One, Two or Three. A lower rate is used for Walk-on One when forty-one or more SAs are called on location on a single day.

**Walk-on One (Under Forty-one SAs)**

| | |
|---|---|
| Day of Attendance/Recording | £66.55 |
| Two Episodes Recorded | £83.30 |
| Three or More Episodes Recorded | £100.05 |

**Walk-on One (Forty-one or more SAs)**

| | |
|---|---|
| Day of Attendance/Recording | £57.10 |
| Two Episodes Recorded | £67.50 |
| Three or More Episodes Recorded | £81.00 |

**Walk-on Two (Non-speaking)**

| | |
|---|---|
| Day of Attendance | £68.25 |
| Two or More Episodes Rehearsed | £102.45 |
| Day of Recording | £86.20 |
| Two or More Episodes Recorded | £129.35 |

**Walk-on Three (Speaking)**

| | |
|---|---|
| Day of Attendance | £68.25 |
| Two or More Episodes Rehearsed | £102.45 |
| Day of Recording | £102.60 |
| Two or More Episodes Recorded | £153.90 |

**Overtime (Single Episode Per Hour)**

| | Day shoot | Night Shoot |
|---|---|---|
| Walk-on One | £12.48 | £18.72 |
| Walk-on One (Over Forty-one SAs) | £10.70 | £16.05 |
| Walk-on Two (Non speaking) | £16.16 | £24.24 |
| Walk-on Three (Speaking) | £19.23 | £28.85 |

**Definitions:**

**Walk-on One:** Shall mean a performer who is not required to give individual characterisation nor to speak any word or line of dialogue, except that crowd noises shall not be deemed to be dialogue in this context.

**Walk-on Two (Non-speaking):** Shall mean a performer not required to give individual characterisation but who is required to impersonate an identifiable individual subject to individual direction.

**Walk-on Three (Speaking):** Shall mean a performer who, in addition to carrying out the function of a Walk-on Two, shall also be required to speak a very few unimportant words where the precise words spoken do not matter.

**Notes:**

Overtime begins after nine working hours (that is ten hours, including one hour unpaid for a meal break).

Payment for night work is paid at one-and-a-half times the appropriate daily rate. If work is scheduled to start before 7am or after midnight, the entire work period attracts night rates. If work extends beyond midnight, but was not previously scheduled to do so, the night rate is applied after midnight only.

A higher pay scale is used on public holidays.

Multi-episodic payments apply if two or more programmes are recorded on a single day.

A slightly lower fee is paid to Walk-on Twos and Walk-on Threes for days of attendance (ie, days where scenes are rehearsed, but no actual filming takes place. A multi-episodic payment is made if more than one episode is rehearsed on such days).

Walk-on Ones do not receive repeat fees, but Walk-on Twos and Threes may be entitled to repeat fees.

Other additional payments are varied and can fall under twenty categories, including early calls, special skills, nudity, costume fittings, travel, auditions and special clothing.

## WHAT YOU COULD EARN UNDER THE EQUITY/TAC WELSH INDEPENDENT TELEVISION AGREEMENT

Similar to the ITV agreement, but with only two grades: Walk-on One and Walk-on Two.

**Walk on One**

| | |
|---|---|
| Higher Daily Rate | £67.00 |
| Minimum Daily Rate | £52.00 |
| Minimum Half Day Rate | £42.00 |

**Walk on Two**

| | |
|---|---|
| Daily Rate | £91.00 |

**Overtime Per Hour**

| | |
|---|---|
| Walk-on One Full Day Rate | £9.75 |
| Walk-on One Higher Day Rate | £12.56 |
| Walk-on Two Daily Rate | £17.06 |

**Definitions:**

**Walk-on One**: Is not required to give individual characterisation, or to speak scripted dialogue, other than crowd noises.

**Walk-on Two**: Is not required to give individual characterisation but may be required to impersonate an identifiable individual and speak a few unimportant words.

**Notes:**

Overtime begins after eight working hours (that is, nine hours including an unpaid hour for a meal break).

Day rates for Walk-on Ones are negotiated above the minimum, depending on experience, skills, discomfort, continuity, length of day and individual direction.

Walk-on Ones are not paid repeat fees, Walk-on Twos receive 100 per cent of the agreed fee per repeat on a UK terrestrial channel (which in Wales also includes S4C).

Other additional fees are varied, and fall under five categories: special skills, costume fittings, costume change, appearance change and demanding work.

## WORKING AS AN ACTOR

All SA and Walk-on agreements only provide for a few, unscripted and unimportant words to be spoken on camera. If you are being asked to do more than that, you should be issued with an Equity actor's contract. Equity has separate actor agreements for PACT television productions and also for cinema films. For more information, ask your agent or contact Equity.

## COMMERCIALS

The current Equity rates for SAs and Walk-ons used in commercials have not been updated for a number of years. Therefore the Equity minimum rates are actually somewhat less than you will probably find yourself earning. If you work as an SA on a commercial then rates do vary, but you can expect to earn between £90 and £150 for a ten-hour day. Overtime is then usually paid at a fifth of the daily rate per hour. Walk-ons on commercials usually earn between £150 and £250 and you can sometimes be paid repeat fees or a buyout.

Getting a more prominent role, and being a featured artiste in a TV commercial can pay very lucratively. Traditionally you would have been paid an agreed daily rate, and then repeat fees for each time it was shown. However, increasingly production companies offer a one-off buyout figure, so they do not have to pay you repeat fees. This buyout is dependent on the length of time the commercial will be seen, and where it will be seen. Buyouts are usually calculated as a percentage amount of the daily rate. Your agent should be able to give you guidance on what these percentages should be for each country an advert will be shown in. These percentages vary due to the size of audience and number of channels. Space does not permit giving illustrations for every country here, but as an example, if your BSF (Basic Shoot Fee) was £250, you could receive a UK buyout for one year of 1,000 per cent of BSF (£2,500). A one year buyout for France might be 400 per cent of BSF (£1,000), while for Greece a year's buyout might be another 100 per cent (£250), so it can soon add up to a tidy amount.

## PHOTOGRAPHIC WORK

Photographic commercial fees depend on how featured you are and the usage of the photo. Generally if you are a featured artiste you will get £100 an hour Basic Shoot Fee and then a buyout of varying percentages depending on the usage (for example, different amounts for press, billboards and Internet usage). Working in the background on a photographic job is paid at a similar rate to Walk-ons in TV commercials. Expect to earn between £150 and £250 for a ten-hour day.

## OTHER TYPES OF JOBS

Certain areas of work are not as well regulated as far as payment is concerned, with no specific union agreements in place. Pop videos and corporate videos are a good example. In these cases the agency's policy on what they consider to be an acceptable fee is the only real influencing factor. For work as an SA on a pop promo expect to earn between £90 and £200 for the day. It is important for you to find out how long that day is, and at what point you will go into any overtime payment, if at all. Fees for corporate videos are also negotiated, and are usually between £90 and £250 depending on what you are expected to do, which can range from basic background work to more involved role-play acting.

## CHARITY JOBS

From time to time you may be asked to do a job for charity (such as Comic Relief) that may be paid at less than the correct rates, or may not be paid at all. This will be the only legitimate time that not being paid the correct rates may be acceptable to you. You are of course under no obligation to accept such work.

## NUDITY

Nudity is something that will crop up from time to time: you could be asked to be a naked body double for an actor, or to be a dead body lying naked in a morgue, or you could even be asked to perform simulated sex. Normally fees for any kind of nudity are negotiated between the production and the agent beforehand — and they are not as much as you might expect! The BBC and ITV Equity agreements do specify a minimum extra payment for partial nudity (around £50). The going rate to appear completely nude or simulate sex in any production is £200 to £500, in addition to your daily rate.

## WAITING TO BE PAID

Waiting to be paid for work is something that you will need to get used to, and you should learn to budget your personal finances accordingly. Do not rely on payments to come in at a set time to pay your personal bills. However, the law does protect you from your agency holding on to your money longer than it should. The agency has to pay you within ten days of receiving the money. Unfortunately, payment by production companies to agencies is not as quick as it should be, and indeed is an area that could do with some attention from the DTI. The industry standard for film and television payment is four to six weeks from the date that you worked to the day you receive the money. However, some companies are more efficient at paying than others (those which make commercials can be particularly bad at paying on time). It is not uncommon to hear complaints about waiting over three months for payment.

There are some legitimate reasons why payment can take a while. A production may have to process hundreds or sometimes thousands of individual payments for any one week, and this can be a very time-consuming process. There are some variations, but the basic procedure is as follows. The production company sends the agency copies of all the salary vouchers for any particular day or, if it is for a job where vouchers were not used, a list with amounts for each artiste. The agency then produces an invoice with all the individual payments and sends it back to the production company. The production company then pays that invoice, sending the agency a cheque for the whole amount. The agency then pays individuals either by cheque, or straight into their bank account, having first deducted their commission.

## WHAT TO DO IF PAYMENT NEVER ARRIVES

If you have a concern, your first contact should be your agent. While it will not be possible for them to pay you until they themselves have been paid, they have a duty to chase the payment on your behalf. If sufficient time has passed without payment (anything over three months) you should take further action by writing to your agent and including photocopies of any proof of work on that day (such as a copy of your signed voucher — always keep the original). If you are a union member, send a copy of the letter to your union as well, as they may be able to put pressure on the agency and, ultimately, on the production company. Be aware that a lot of independent productions wind up their activity as a company three to six months after the end of shooting, so don't leave it too long or the production company may no longer exist. Your final avenue may be to take legal advice and go to the small claims court.

## TAX IMPLICATIONS

Whilst working as a Supporting Artiste the Inland Revenue will probably treat you as self-employed, and therefore you will not normally have Income Tax deducted from your remittance. This is *not* the same as not paying tax, of course! You should fill in a tax return at the end of each financial year. The tax office is very strict in the film business. Don't assume you can get away without paying tax — they *will* catch up with you. The best thing to do is open a separate bank account, and pay a portion of each job into it. That way it won't be so tricky to find the money for your tax bill when it arrives. National Insurance is more complex with regard to Supporting Artistes, and the Inland Revenue are in something of a muddle themselves as to whether Class One National Insurance should be deducted from your remittance or not. As of writing, this is under review, but expect National Insurance to be deducted from your remittance by production companies until they are told to do otherwise.

# TAKING IT FURTHER

So, you've been working as an SA for a while, you're enjoying it, and you want to take it further. How can you increase your chances of being offered more jobs, and what are the options if your sights are set on more than standard background work? As well as answering these questions, this chapter will also highlight some pitfalls to look out for along the way.

## HOW TO GET WORK AS A WALK-ON

After becoming an experienced SA and getting a taste for the action, you may decide you would like a bit more of a challenge. Perhaps you feel confident enough to do a Walk-on or small feature, but how do you get cast in those roles? There are three ways to get work as a Walk-on. The first is down to luck — simply being in the right place at the right time. If you've got the right look on set, it's quite normal to be upgraded from the background on the day.

The second is to get your agent to book you as a Walk-on in the first place. This is a tricky thing to achieve. Firstly your agent needs to be able to trust that you can act and perform well. Therefore, if you have worked as a Walk-on before, make sure you tell your agent that, and if possible send them a tape so they can see for themselves what a good performer you are. Once they have used you once and everything has gone well, they will be more confident about suggesting you in the future.

The third way is to go to a casting or audition, but for this your agent still needs to put you forward. The first thing to do here is to let them know that you want to be put forward for Walk-on roles. They may be wrongly assuming that you are only interested in doing background work, if that is all you've ever done. If your agent knows you're keen and can trust you to behave professionally, they may be willing to take a chance on you.

Some castings are very straightforward. The Casting Director or AD will ask you your name, a few conversational questions, take some pictures and let you go. Other castings can be a little more involved. What should you do if you are asked to perform? You may not have been given prior warning, so the golden rule is to be ready to improvise or read from a script at *any* casting. If you've never done any drama training, don't be put off. Listen carefully to the scenario and then give it one hundred per cent in terms of effort and concentration. You may think you're awful, but you would be surprised by how many SAs, having never performed at a casting before, are given Walk-on roles. Don't be over the top, though. Inexperienced performers often make the mistake of thinking greater enthusiasm makes for better acting. Sometimes less is more.

To give you a fuller picture, here's an SA's experience of castings:

It's like an exam: the better you feel it went, the worse you probably did. And vice versa. Castings are like looking for a contact lens in the dark, and not knowing if you've found it until days later. I never feel as though the production really wants me to know what they're after. They put on their best friendly smiles and tell me to relax, but I always think that they'll laugh at the results with the rest of the team once I've gone. Or maybe it's just me...

I once went to a casting for a Walk-on in a TV advert. As usual, I knew next to nothing about what would be required, so I sat in the waiting area with my senses keening to pick up the least titbit of information that might give me the edge over my competitors. A gaggle of girls who were clearly friends went in one after the other, and came out talking about how they'd been asked if they would mind taking their clothes off.

This was not the kind of information I was expecting. Some girls had said yes, they would be willing to on the day, a couple had baulked at the idea. The worst kind of 'casting couch' urban legends sprang to mind as I sat, terrified, waiting for my name to be called. When my turn came I was asked in with a couple of other hopefuls. We were asked a totally benign series of questions, and participated in a 'party guest' vignette. That was it. (These things are nearly always over before you realise they've begun.) There was no mention of nudity.

It turned out that the girls who had gone in before me were actresses auditioning for the lead role in the advert, and no mere walk-on. I got the walk-on, and one of the other girls got the lead. Sure enough, she had to do a scene in which her bath towel falls down, but it was all very tastefully done. Still, I was happy to leave that sort of thing to the pros.

Laura Tilly

## TEN TIPS FOR A CASTING OR AUDITION

1 Get a good night's sleep the night before — you need to look and feel at your best.

2 Find out from your agent the kind of character being cast (eg. businessman) and dress accordingly if possible.

3 Be natural, don't be too nervous and don't speak too fast. Smile and be yourself.

4 Before you go in, give yourself five minutes just to relax.

5 Listen carefully to what you are being asked to do, and make sure you understand before you start.

6 Don't be afraid to ask questions, but don't talk too much.

7 If you make a mistake, don't give up. Compose yourself and carry on.

8 Give it 100 per cent. You may not be what they're looking for, but if *you* don't believe you are going to get it, you definitely won't.

9 Be confident. If you feel confident and the Casting Director gets that impression, they won't worry about you being nervous on set.

**10** Don't overact. Subtlety can be important!

Keeping these tips in mind, and with a bit of luck, you'll have a good chance of getting a Walk-on or featured role in a production. Here are some examples of SAs who did just that, beginning with a magic 'right place, right time' story...

I booked in at the studio, and according to my salary voucher I was to take part as a spectator in the Quidditch scenes in *Harry Potter and the Chamber of Secrets*. I was waiting on the set, ready to join the others in the grandstand, when I was suddenly asked to go to another set, to see Chris Columbus — the Director. He wanted someone older to take over a Walk-on part that had been originally offered to another Supporting Artiste, and I was accepted.

I was to be the front person carrying a stretcher. The rehearsals for the scene had already taken place, so I was simply shown which bed I had to walk to in the hospital ward set. While we were waiting for the shoot, I took the opportunity to discuss our part of the scene with John, my fellow stretcher-bearer. We were going to be working with some of the stars of the film: Richard Harris, Maggie Smith and Gemma Jones.

I had to follow quickly behind Richard Harris, being careful not to tread on the very long cloak he was wearing! Then, when the 'body' was moved onto the bed, we had to hurriedly leave the ward with our stretcher, and go out of camera shot. Luckily, we did it perfectly time after time, without a hitch. This was the first occasion I'd been in such an important scene. I was thrown in the deep end rather, but proved that I could do it!

**Albert Ratcliffe**

Being told I'd look good dead isn't one of the nicest compliments that I've ever received, but when you're being chosen for a featured part on *London's Burning*, you *do* take it as a great compliment. £65 a day may not have been quite enough danger money though, as the Director explained my character would be trapped in a burning building, hit by a small-scale explosion and dragged half alive by a fireman to safety, only to take part in an emotional resuscitation scene which would sadly fail — and I thought I was just in for a 'walk past and look horrified' kind of day!

With hair covered in rubble, lips painted blue and clothes torn apart by the blast, I wasn't looking my most glamorous as I sheltered from the cold in a hired ambulance, waiting for my scene. Being confined to the inside of an ambulance was a great way to spend the afternoon though, as a couple of other featured Extras and I tried out the gas masks and neck braces. And here's a handy hint I learned: it's quite difficult to get into a body bag and zip yourself up from the inside.

So, the end is nigh and I face my final curtain, as the paramedic places a blanket over the top of my head and pronounces me dead. My Extra life flashes before me — hours sitting on a bench in Albert Square; making serious decisions in the *Coronation Street* canteen (should I go for the cheesecake or the apple pie?) and the relief of a free stomach as the dresser unbuttons your corset after a day filming a BBC costume drama. But nothing compares to the thrill of seeing yourself die on screen. Lucy Wallis: *London's Burning* Extra RIP!

**Lucy Wallis**

---

"Can you all sit on these bean bags looking extremely uncomfortable whilst working in the office?" was the request from the 2nd AD. Not difficult when the night before filming, the women had been told to wear skirts and heels. The first time I flopped into a bean bag my skirt ripped and then, whilst trying to cover acres of American Tan thigh, I got cramp. I couldn't get up for laughing. "That's great!" cried the Director. "Can you do that again for the camera?"

The next minute, it was make-up, change of wardrobe, lighting and props and I became a feature as the biggest bum in BT's Bean Bag ad. When I mentioned that I could also touch-type eighty words a minute I got a close-up typing — and became a one-take wonder to boot!

**Stephanie Barrows**

Being featured in a production does have financial benefits, but there is also a certain amount of personal satisfaction at being chosen from the thousands of others in the casting book — even if it is just because you are the only person with one leg or hairy hands.

However, as you *are* a professional, you tend to act cool and detached on set and suppress any real feelings of excitement. This is particularly true when filming a Walk-on part with a major star. Thus, you find yourself in an extraordinary situation where you are standing in a lift together, but not conversing or really even acknowledging each other. A difficult balance has to be reached where you are not seeming rude, but at the same time not interrupting the actor's 'preparation'.

It is, however, apparently *not* possible to stifle this excitement when eventually seeing the film. In my case, I was in the lift with Robert Redford and, as the film *Spy Game* was nearing its end, I was convinced that my feature — the one I'd told all my friends about — had been cut. Suddenly, the lift doors opened on screen and there I was, twenty feet tall. I'm sure the packed cinema audience must have wondered why I involuntarily leapt to my feet screaming "Yessss!"

**Philip Harvey**

## IMPROVE YOUR CHANCES

With so much competition from fellow SAs, it is very difficult to 'get an edge', and make yourself more attractive than others to Bookers, ADs and Casting Directors. Chapter 3 suggested ways to help make sure Bookers often pick you for jobs. Here are some other tips you can take advantage of to make yourself more useable as an SA.

### Extend Your Wardrobe

It is true that many productions make or source their own costumes, but your versatility and 'marketability' as an SA can be improved by extending your own wardrobe, particularly for present-day productions. Imagine that your agent has a job that requires a business suit, and they've narrowed it down to a choice of two SAs. They're not sure about the other artiste, but know that you can cover the requirements with your own clothes. Congratulations — you've just got the job! It's also worth noting that providing special clothing can sometimes mean you will be entitled to an additional payment.

Certain scenarios come up all the time in background work and there-fore the more stereotypes you can conform to, the more scenarios you could be used for — and the more work you will get. But don't forget that your ability to be used can also depend on whether you are 'ordinary' or 'extraordinary'-looking (see Chapter 1) and this can affect which items you chose to add to your wardrobe.

Formal evening functions are a common scenario. To help you get chosen for these scenes, men should get hold of a tuxedo, and women should have at least one long formal evening gown and one shorter cocktail dress. Avoid anything that may upset the camera — no garish colours or patterns. If you can't afford to buy new, charity shops are a good option.

Business wear is another common request. If you are generally per-ceived as an 'ordinary' clean-cut, smart-looking person you could be cast as a business-person. However, you won't be used as a business-type if you only have one tatty old suit, so it may well be worth invest-ing in a good business suit. Props are also useful — a briefcase and umbrella, for example.

Other clothing briefs can relate to specific social functions and events, such as a morning suit for weddings or sporting kit like gym wear, football kit, horse riding gear or tennis whites. The types of clothes required are less specific, but other common scenarios to think about include airport or railway station scenes, courtroom scenes, and club-bing, bar, pub or restaurant scenes. 'Extraordinary' types should also arm themselves with the tools of the trade. If you resemble a mean-looking bouncer, get yourself a smart black suit, so you can also be used as a doorman at posh parties, or as a bodyguard.

### Uniforms

The uniforms most frequently seen on screen are those of nurses, the police and paramedics. Be aware though, the only uniforms that will be useful in your wardrobe are real ones — you won't be used as a nurse if your 'uniform' looks like a stripper's costume. You may have a uniform as part of your current job or from a previous occupation, for example if you served in the military. Please note however that it is actually illegal for members of the public to buy real police, fire serv-ice or paramedic uniforms.

## Other Costumes

You may think that your eighteenth century battle re-enactment costume or your genuine Beefeater uniform may not ever be relevant, and you would probably be right. However, if you do have anything unusual it's still worth mentioning to your agent. You never know what you could be asked for. Vicars and clowns are always needed. If your family is from outside the UK, traditional ethnic dress may be useful — Chinese, Japanese and African costumes are often requested.

Your body can sometimes be a costume. People covered in piercings or tattoos are in regular demand. Maybe you have a toe or finger missing, or you can take your teeth out, or you are an odd shape or size. Don't be shy, all of these things and more have been asked for, and you should make sure your agent knows about anything that could help get you a job!

## Cars and Bikes

Occasionally you may be asked to provide and drive a car on set. Again, this is a good way of earning an additional payment. Non-distinctive is the key here. If you are buying a new car, make sure it is not red or white; these colours stand out too much on camera and will not be used. Private number-plates or very flash cars tend to stand out too much as well.

If a specialist vehicle is required, specific companies that have special insurance usually provide them. However, there is always a demand for black cabs, pushbikes and motorbikes. If you ride a motorbike, get yourself a despatch bag — you could be used to play a courier.

## SPECIAL SKILLS

Generally, you either have a special skill or you don't. It really is not worth pretending you can do something and then wasting everyone's time on the day. There is nothing more embarrassing for you, and your agent, than to be asked to go to a casting for, say, speaking fluent French, when actually your 'French' is limited to enjoying a bottle of Bordeaux now and then. If you are not confident enough to perform a skill on camera in front of the crew, then don't mention it.

## SPECIAL SKILLS: LET YOUR AGENT KNOW!

Under certain agreements you may be paid more if you are asked to perform a specific skill. You should tell your agent if any of the following apply to you:

**1** You can speak a foreign language competently. ❑

**2** You can play any particular sport to a high standard. ❑

**3** You can play any musical instrument to a high standard. ❑

**4** You can sing (in tune). ❑

**5** You are a trained dancer. ❑

**6** You have any circus skills. ❑

**7** You are a trained marksman. ❑

**8** You have been in the military. ❑

**9** You are comfortable with appearing nude. ❑

**10** Your profession involves a skill that may be seen on screen, ie, paramedic, masseuse or stenographer. ❑

**11** You have an unusual hobby that could be used on camera, eg, part-time contortionist or balloon modeller. ❑

Any special skills you have could lead to a greatly enhanced role on a production, behind the camera as well as in front of it. Here's an example of an SA who has benefited from his specialist military knowledge:

Of the more unusual skills I've been called to use was camel riding, while shooting the period war drama *The Four Feathers* on location in Morocco. I'll never forget riding across the desert as dawn broke. I also assisted the make-up team, helped the storyboard artist with some ideas, and was a drill and weapons instructor and crowd marshal.

Just one day saw me acting as military advisor for a scene to the director Shekhar Kapur and 1st AD Tommy Gormley, and advising actors Wes Bentley, Mike Sheen and Kris Marshall on their particular actions. This being done whilst sitting on a camel, dressed as a Victorian soldier, two-way radio in one hand, mobile phone in the other to liaise with the Military Co-ordinator Henry Camilleri, and a radio mike strapped to my chest. I was just working out how to jump off the camel at a particular point for the scene, thinking things couldn't get much more complicated, when Tommy Gormley strode up. "Richard sir, a bit of dialogue for you in this!"

For the HBO series *Band of Brothers* I spent three great weeks bouncing around in a sixty year-old Cromwell as a tank commander, both on and off screen. One day a new SA turned up to play a tank commander, but he had no previous experience with tanks. We politely explained there was no way we could let him actually command, as it is does take skill and practice to safely guide a vehicle like that through a crowd of potentially hundreds of people, but that he was welcome to go along for the ride. At the end of the first take he shook his head and said, "I couldn't have done that. You were talking to me, the driver and the production almost simultaneously, with people running everywhere, *and* you were acting at the same time!"

**Richard Manlove**

## BE AWARE OF OTHER TRAPS

With competition intense, SAs often look for ways to become more useable than everyone else. By all means, improve your CV by including any Walk-ons or small features you have done, but be very careful about doing anything that is going to cost you more money.

### Show Reels

If you think you're a good performer and you've got a few Walk-ons under your belt, you may consider putting together a show reel of your work. With today's technology this is probably something you could put together yourself fairly cheaply, with a couple of video recorders and the right connection leads. If you do go to a company to have a show reel compiled professionally, you are likely to be charged a lot of money.

## Model Cards and Ten By Eights

Having a 'z card' made, or new ten by eight photos printed may be a good way of showing your agent that you can look different from the image they have of you. Nevertheless, this is an expensive process, and may not make any difference. If you are not sure, ask your agent if they think it is worthwhile.

## Acting Classes

If you are going to spend money on acting classes, make sure you are enrolling on a legitimate course that has a reputation and a qualification you can use on your CV. There are some acting classes that are expensive and give you a certificate. However, after you've been going for ten weeks and have spent the best part of £500, you may find out that the certificate means nothing to anyone except yourself.

A less expensive first step may be to join your local amateur dramatics society. If that goes well then consider acting classes. The major problem with acting is that you need to have the seed of talent to be nurtured in the first place; if you can't act, no amount of expensive classes will help. So be self-critical, and ask those around you what they think of your performances.

## Getting an Acting Agent

It is possible to make the leap from SA to actor, but it is rare and can be a very daunting prospect. The process of getting an acting agent is similar to that of getting an SA agent — sending out lots of CVs and photos to reputable companies and hoping to be called in for an interview — but with far fewer artistes on their books, it's much more difficult to be taken on by an acting agent. The major problem is that once you *do* get one, the first thing they will tell you to do is, "Stop doing background work!" All too often I've spoken to SAs who have told me they can't do background work any more, because they now have an acting agent, but six months later are begging for SA work because despite numerous castings they haven't had a single acting job. They obviously have some talent, otherwise the acting agent would not have taken them on, but perhaps they would have spent their time more wisely building their CVs with Walk-ons and small features booked through their SA agent.

In the last five years I have come into contact with more than 10,000 different Supporting Artistes, of which I have counted only five that have made the step from SA to full-time, recognisable working actor. Therefore it is possible, but the odds are stacked against you. That said, if you are given the opportunity to make the leap from SA to actor, give it a go, but if it doesn't work out don't be too proud to go back to working as an SA. After all, you have to eat and pay the bills.

## OTHER STRINGS TO YOUR BOW

As well as the different genres and media you could work in, there are also different types of jobs you could be asked to do other than Supporting Artiste. Some SAs work as look-alikes or doubles. Some get jobs as actors' Stand-ins. Some supplement their incomes by doing voiceovers as well as background work.

### Look-alikes and Doubling

If you are lucky enough (or unlucky, depending on how you look at it) to resemble someone famous, you could be asked to double an actor. Everyone has a *doppelgänger* and famous people are no different. Some SAs make their main income from looking like someone else, and there are even a handful of specialist look-alike agencies. But be aware that sometimes those who *think* they look like a famous person, don't. Conversely, artistes are sometimes shocked when they get a call telling them that they are the spitting image of a famous actor.

Doubling in film and TV is more about being the same age, skin tone and body size, and having similar hair to the actor than having a startling resemblance. (Indeed, if you are particularly short, you could be used as a double for a child actor.) It is then up to the skill of the make-up artist to make you look the same. With the right hair-style and an identical costume, you will be indistinguishable from the actor in certain types of shots — and that's the idea. Doubles are used much more than you might imagine — if the star of a film is seen in  longshot, or conversely in a close-up where his or her face isn't visible, chances are it's actually their double you're looking at. This kind of doubling is not something you have any control over and you really have to wait to be asked, but if you think you are a good double for an actor, it's worth letting your agent know. (Please note that being this kind of double is quite separate from being a stunt double. In an action film, the stars will often have their own stunt doubles as well.)

Here's another 'right place, right time' story, this one from an SA who suddenly found himself doubling, lending a hand in the making of a big-budget movie:

Perhaps my greatest performance in six years as a Supporting Artiste was being cast as Pierce Brosnan's hand in the Bond film *Tomorrow Never Dies*. Due to the Thai authorities blocking a major stunt sequence (the pyrotechnic destruction of a helicopter), Eon Productions, masterminds of Bond on film, were forced to recreate the location on a disused air base in Hertfordshire.

The scene was set — Bond rips a washing line holder off the wall of a house (made entirely of plywood of course) and hurls it into the manically whirring rotors of the attacking helicopter (which in fact had no rotors at all and was dangling precariously from a crane. Sorry if I'm spoiling the dream!). However, Bond himself was not there, as Pierce Brosnan had better things to do than turn up for the filming of a cutaway shot during a stunt scene. (I always noted his attendance on the days love scenes were shot, however. Funny that!) That left Brosnan's stunt double to fill in for the close-up of Bond's arm ripping the washing line down. Not for long though. A shriek of horror was heard as the 1st AD noticed the tattoo on the stunt double's hand, something the suave 007 would of course never have. After a quick kangaroo court-style dismissal of the stuntman, it was decided to patrol for a new hand.

Fire officers, caterers, even a strange bloke who just happened to be hanging around, all thrust their hands forward in a desperate attempt to double everyone's favourite secret agent. But it is patience and suitability that pay dividends in the film game, and as everyone's hopeful pinkies were rejected on the basis of nail quality, I buffed, clipped and cleaned. My reward was to be captured on celluloid.

It is a legacy I will treasure always and forward to generations new, for I was indeed James Bond's hand for the day.

Jos Dewing

## Standing In

A Stand-in is a person used to physically take the place of an actor during the often lengthy time it takes to set up the lighting and camera positions for a scene, leaving the actor free to rehearse elsewhere (or perhaps just relax in his trailer!). As with doubles, the Stand-in usually has a similar height, age, hairstyle and skin tone to the actor in question, but as they will not actually be appearing on screen, a really close resemblance is less important. Sometimes a production will use the same person to stand in *and* double for an actor, but this is not the norm. On lower budget productions, a Utility Stand-in might cover three or four different actors during the course of filming.

Productions require a huge amount of time and energy from their Stand-ins, but the rewards are good, in that you are really treated as part of the crew. Normally a Stand-in is required every day of the production, so the financial rewards can be very good as well. Often, SAs who have done one Stand-in job tell their agent they don't want to do background work any more. This is a mistake. It is certainly true that a small number of Stand-ins in the business are used repeatedly, but you have to be *very* lucky to find yourself working as a Stand-in all the time. So it's worth keeping your options open by taking background jobs when Stand-in work is thin on the ground. Here's what working as a Stand-in has been like for a couple of Supporting Artistes:

Being a Stand-in is generally much harder work than straightforward background, as you have to be on set at all times. At least with background, you can relax when you're not required in the 'holding area' you've been designated (green room, coach, bus, toilet, etc).

A couple of Stand-in jobs I have done spring to mind mainly because of their diversity. I should first point out that as well as being a struggling actor, I am also a musician. So, one sunny day on location in a field in Hertfordshire my mobile rang. Not a problem normally, but on this occasion I had great difficulty reaching it underneath the cumbersome costume I was wearing. I eventually located it. It turned out to be a call from a pleasant-sounding chap named Kevin Locke. Kevin explained that he was the bandleader of one of the top Abba tribute bands (the Real Abba Gold) and they were looking for a new 'Benny'. Unfortunately my mobile signal was weak and I misunderstood him. I thought he was the Casting Director for the revamped *Crossroads*... wrong Benny!

However, I said that I was interested but would have to call him back because I was dressed as sheepdog! A stunt sheepdog to be precise!! Kevin laughed nervously. I was in fact standing in for Barry from the Chuckle Brothers on an episode of the kids' show *Chucklevision*. (The Chuckles are the nicest pair of chaps you could ever meet, by the way. I worked with them three years later and when Paul, the other one, saw me he immediately said, "It's the sheepdog!")

Meanwhile, back to Kevin Locke. The next call I received from Kevin, he really must have thought I was taking the Mickey! This time I explained that I would have to call him back (again) because I was dangling off a nuclear reactor in a submarine that had crashed vertically into the ocean bed.

It was true, though. I was standing in for Robert Carlyle (we are the same height, five foot six) who was playing the baddie in the James Bond film *The World is Not Enough*. Kevin soon realized that I wasn't winding him up, and happily I got the job with his band!

**Lindsay Elliott**

---

When I first signed up to an agency, the phone rang within two days, and suddenly I was standing next to Glenn Close on a movie set. Then two months later I was part of a football crowd in a chocolate bar ad. But then six months passed, and despite many four-hour journeys to endless little studios for castings, the phone had stopped ringing.

The trouble is, I'm six foot seven inches in bare feet, and this seemed to be working against me — in most crowd shots, I'd only be visible from the neck down! The phone finally rang: would I like to work on a film about a certain boy wizard, as the Stand-in for a famous actor and comedian who also happened to be six foot seven? Well, I'd loved the books, and the chance to meet the man who I'd admired since he'd first done his funny walks thirty years earlier filled me with childish anticipation.

Yes — I stood in for John Cleese in *Harry Potter*. Despite warnings from others that you shouldn't speak to him, or get in his way, or generally make a nuisance of yourself, I found Cleese to be a really nice, down-to-earth bloke. We even did *The Guardian* crossword together. Eager to impress, I sneaked off and phoned my father, who always completes *The Guardian* crossword, to glean some answers to impress the man. Unfortunately, Dad's paper boy had delivered *The Times* that day, so I was stuffed from the word go.

The whole Potter process was fantastic, and we even got to play football all day because a camera had broken, and a man had to come from Milan to fix it. The harness they strapped me into (so I could float about like Cleese's ghostly character) hurt like hell, and it is true that Mr Cleese got paid considerably more money than I did, even though I worked many more hours — but I loved every minute. It's just a shame John Cleese doesn't make films more often!

Mike Jones

## Becoming Part of the Crew

Several of the established Assistant Directors and other crew members currently working in the UK started their careers as Supporting Artistes. So if you really fall in love with being on set, this could be an option. Bear in mind it is incredibly competitive, and you will need to start at the bottom. As Chapter 4 showed, the film business operates a strict hierarchy, and the people at the bottom work harder and longer for less. Working as a runner, you are the first person to arrive on set and the last person to leave, and the chances are you will actually earn less money than you would working as an SA. However, if you have the commitment, energy and stamina, it is possible to work your way up.

## Voiceover Artists

Voiceovers are the voice you hear over the top of a TV advert, radio advert or animation, or providing commentary for a documentary. If you think you have a good voice, this could be another avenue to explore. Again, specialist agencies exist that only offer voices to productions (a few are listed at the back of the book). This is a tough area to crack, and it's very rare for SAs to move into it, though not impossible. Many ads use recognisable actors for their voiceovers, and competition is high. You will need to have a show reel recorded professionally, which could be expensive. Before you splash out, ask yourself: is there anything unique about your voice (other than that you like the sound of it)? Do you have a strong accent for example, or is your voice particularly deep?

## Becoming a Stunt Performer

If you are the daring kind, and have a lot of the right skills, you could consider stunt work. To work as a Stunt Performer you need to get yourself included on the Stunt Register. To do this you must have completed sixty days in front of the camera, as well as demonstrate skills in five different disciplines:

## STUNT DISCIPLINES

1 Fighting techniques, such as martial arts or boxing.

2 Falling techniques, such as trampolining or high diving.

3 Horse riding and driving skills.

4 Showing agility and strength, such as gymnastics or rock climbing.

5 Water skills, such as swimming or diving.

Once you get on the register, you will spend three years as a probationary member before becoming a fully qualified Stunt Performer. A word of caution: with changes in technology and special effects, stunt performance is becoming a dying trade. Big feature films that would once have had dozens of Stunt Performers, will now only employ a handful, as the rest of the work is done with computers in post production. Training is also very expensive, so think about it carefully before going ahead. That said, I have known a few SAs who have made the transition to Stunt Performer. For further information about getting on the Stunt Register, contact Equity (address in the appendices).

## Provide a Filming Location

If you own a particularly interesting house or building that holds architectural value, it may be possible to rent it out to production companies as a location. Bear in mind that this will mean your property being totally overrun with cast and crew, but if you can put up with that, they will be contractually obliged to leave it in the same state they found it. A good starting point for this may be to talk to your local film commission. There are twenty-one different commissions around the UK, which often help productions find the right locations — contact the British Film Commission to find the nearest one to you (details at the back of the book).

## Becoming a Child Chaperone

Whenever children under sixteen are required for filming, they have to be accompanied by a chaperone, who makes sure they arrive safely and watches over them during the filming day. Chaperones are usually paid at the same rate as adult SAs. Contact the educational welfare officer of the local borough council where you live for an application form.

## OVER-EXPOSURE

Recently an AD asked me to replace someone I had booked because "they look too much like an Extra". I thought about this for a while and realised they didn't mean that. What they actually meant was that they had seen that person too often before. It is unfortunately true, with a limited number of people making the casting decisions, that you can become recognisable, and be seen too much. A major part of being an SA is the ability to blend into the background. If you start to become too recognised this may work against you. Therefore it is worth bearing in mind that if you've been busily working as an SA for a number of years and don't seem to get as much work as you used to, this could be the reason.

Another reason may be that you are not as patient and flexible as you once were. There is nothing worse for an AD than hearing the line: "I've been in the business for thirty years and it's not how it used to be." The chances are, it is exactly how it used to be, but you are not. If you regard yourself as a 'professional' SA, then make sure you act like one. Being a know-it-all and becoming a nuisance will not make anyone want to use you. The crew are looking to you to be friendly, responsive and alert. Offering them advice on how to do their jobs will not be taken well. Doing a job for a really long time doesn't necessarily make you better at doing that job. One AD asks me to only use people who are new to the game, as he finds them much more excited by the experience, and therefore much more helpful. That is not to say that if you've been an SA for a while, you should give up. There are some really good 'professionals' who get asked for by name, because they know how to behave, and work as team leaders within the crowd. But if you become the one who is always complaining, or you're not enjoying it as much as you used to, maybe it's time to look for another job.

# REGIONAL AND INTERNATIONAL VARIATIONS

## LONDON AND THE SOUTH EAST

It is fair to say that in the UK, most SA work is focused around London and the South East. There is a logical reason for this: most production companies are based in the South East, and as a result most of the technicians are based there too. The major film studios in the UK have a long history, stretching back over seventy years, and pretty much all of them are in the South East. The main ones are Shepperton Studios in Middlesex and Pinewood Studios in Buckinghamshire. Other big studios in the region are Elstree, Leavesden, Ealing, Bray, Greenford, Teddington and Twickenham. East and West London also have a concentration of smaller studios. In and around London, locations are often used near to the studio where the production is based. A full list of the major studios in the country (with addresses) can be found at the back of the book.

## THE REST OF THE UK

What if you don't live in the South East? Outside of London, some other major cities offer concentrated areas of work, and there are Supporting Artiste agencies based in the regions (there's a list of established ones in the appendices). You may think that you live in a region where filming never occurs. While it is true that some areas are used far more than others, most places have seen film crews descend on them at one time or another. Think of pretty much any part of the country, and you can usually come up with a film or TV series that was based there: *Inspector Morse* in Oxford, *Spender* and *Get Carter* in Newcastle, *The Full Monty* in Sheffield, *Lovejoy* in Suffolk and East Anglia and *Poldark* and *Wycliffe* in Cornwall, to give a few random examples.

## BRISTOL AND THE SOUTH WEST

The BBC does quite a lot of filming in the Bristol area, most famously with *Casualty* (though its spinoff, *Holby City*, is shot in London). The Channel 4 drama *Teachers* was also filmed in Bristol. Feature films often use the beautiful scenery found in the South West for location shoots. Sometimes blockbusters also pay a visit: in 2002 for example, the James Bond movie *Die Another Day* shot a sequence in Cornwall.

## THE MIDLANDS AND THE NORTH

Nottingham is the home of Carlton's television studios, and Birmingham has a lot of production activity. Manchester and Liverpool are famous for *Coronation Street* (filmed at Granada Studios) and *Brookside* respectively, and Leeds is the home of Yorkshire Television studios, with *Emmerdale* filmed nearby. Along with this regular work, many other TV series are made in this part of the country, from *Peak Practice* (and now its replacement *Sweet Medicine*) which films in Derbyshire, to the neverending sitcom *Last of the Summer Wine*, which returns each year to shoot in and around the West Yorkshire town of Holmfirth. Here's an SA's view of working in the North (and it goes without saying that you should follow his advice!):

The actual job differs little if you are working as an Extra up North, but the pay is much better in London, where the Equity members are far more militant. The BBC and Granada up here honour Union rates, but the independent film companies are absolute pirates, and will pay as little as they can get away with. They know that Liverpool, Newcastle and Dublin are deprived areas, and scale down accordingly. A certain multi-million dollar thriller that shot in Liverpool recently destroyed six very expensive cars in the name of art; the Extras, however, were paid £50 a day. Some productions will even ask you to work for nothing, on the understanding that if the film makes money in the future, you will receive your true reward. They never do make any money, of course (and who's going to tell you if they do?). The moral of the story is, *never* give your services for free. The problem is that there are always many people who are so dazzled by the glitter and tinsel of showbiz, they will take a day off work just to be in a TV series or feature film, for nothing.

Ron Harrison

## SCOTLAND, IRELAND AND WALES

Scottish TV dramas are on the increase, and go a little further than just the Glasgow-based *Taggart* — a recent example being the BBC's *Monarch of the Glen*, which shoots in the Badenoch and Strathspey area of the Highlands. Since the advent of *Trainspotting*, more and more feature films have based themselves in Scotland. There are also plans to build major film studio complexes in Edinburgh (backed by Sean Connery) and Glasgow, though progress towards actual construction has been slow, leaving the projects in doubt. The Irish government seems to give more tax incentives to companies filming there. For this reason, productions that might have been filmed in the UK can be attracted towards the Republic of Ireland (for example, the Scottish epic *Braveheart* was actually shot mostly in Ireland, as it was far cheaper than Scotland!) Wales produces a fair number of Welsh-language dramas and soaps, mostly based around Cardiff. Films shot in Wales over the years range from *Twin Town* to *Jabberwocky*, while both *Inn of the Sixth Happiness* and the legendary *Carry On Up the Khyber* used Snowdonia to stand in for the Himalayas.

## OPPORTUNITIES TO WORK ABROAD

A lot of British and American-backed films shoot part of their schedules abroad. This may be to film scenes in a particular location, or it could be a way of saving money. The overall cost of filming is much lower in eastern parts of Europe and in countries like Morocco than in the UK. If crowds are being cast locally, there is a possibility of being used if you are brave, and just turn up 'on spec'. Some SAs have done this — arriving in a country where they know filming to be taking place. (Be aware though that unless it's a country in the European Union, you'll need the right paperwork, namely a work permit obtained before you travel from the embassy of the country concerned.) Although good fun if you are the travelling kind, it is rarely financially rewarding — the local wages may be considerably lower than in the UK. A production will not pay for SAs to fly to a specific country, or pay for accommodation, if they can find what they need locally. With living expenses included it could even cost *you* money to get work in this way.

Occasionally productions will fly in Supporting Artistes if their local resources do not offer them the look, or specific skills, they need. For *Spy Game*, we cast a team of Vietnamese men from London, who were flown out to Morocco to film a Vietnam war sequence. *The Four Feathers* used experienced horse riders and soldiers from the UK while filming in the desert in Morocco. *Captain Correlli's Mandolin* took British soldiers out to Greece, and on *Gladiator*, the background gladiators in the arena were cast in the UK and flown out to the Coliseum set in Malta. Also on *Gladiator*, a five-ball juggler couldn't be found anywhere in Malta, so the production flew one in from London. These instances are rare, so you really have to wait to be asked. However, when they do happen, the production company will arrange any necessary paperwork, pay for your flights and accommodation, and probably also give you the additional daily spending allowance paid to the crew, called 'per diems'.

Sometimes a small UK crew will relocate to a foreign location just for a few days, perhaps so the Second Unit can get some 'establishing' footage for scenes which, though they are set in another country, will actually be shot mostly in the UK. Such filming can often involve the use of doubles:

I was offered the chance to do some doubling work in France on a BBC production (*Ella and The Mothers* starring Michelle Collins). Thus I found myself, (after a brief stop to get three inches lopped off my hair), in Portsmouth, in the early hours of the morning, driving a sports car onto the ferry, on camera. Eventually, we all crossed to Normandy and there ensued three mad days of shooting. The work I was given was long and hard but varied, from being filmed sleeping in a car on a beach in -4°F, to being shot driving up and down a French motorway for hours on end (including pulling a few U-turns past some very surprised French farmers). The whole trip was exhausting, but enjoyable too, and I would definitely do it all again, given the chance.

I would say that the main difference on a shoot abroad like this is that you become part of the crew. On a UK shoot, any Extra will tell you that, generally, it's an 'us and them' situation. Abroad though, you don't just work with the cast and crew; you eat, drink, play cards and sing raucous bar songs with them. Like me, you may find that the cast and crew will party as hard as they work, and you won't get much sleep. Fun yes, but on the flip side, always remember that you must remain professional at all times, alcohol and sleep deprivation are no excuse, and when it comes to the shoot — be punctual, be reliable and be productive. My advice: if you want your time abroad to be enjoyable, be sociable, well-mannered, patient, relaxed — and don't forget to buy a round now and then!

**Kerry-ann Willing**

Opportunities to work abroad come up more regularly for commercials, particularly within the European Union. It is not uncommon for a commercial to shoot in, say, Paris, Brussels or Madrid. Production companies will then fly out artistes for the shoot, and pay for flights and accommodation. Quite often it's because the specific types of performers cannot be found locally. Here's an example:

> I was sent by my agent for a casting to play the character Hercule Poirot in an advert (someone had said I resembled David Suchet, the actor who has famously played him for years). When I got there the room was full of Poirots of all shapes and sizes, some in full costume — very pro! When it was my turn in front of the Casting Director, I slipped off my raincoat, took my little Poirot moustache out of my pocket and stuck it under my nose. Giving a quick profile left and right for the camera, I muttered some French-type gibberish, thanked them for seeing me and I was gone!
>
> Four days later my agent rang to inform me that I'd got the job. "Great!" I said. "Where is it?" "Denmark," she said. "Denmark Street?" I asked. "No, Copenhagen!" "Fine, fax me the details," I said, as if this happened every day. The job was a commercial for Tele Danmark, a company similar to our BT. I was flown out to Copenhagen on a Friday night, met at the airport and taken to a posh hotel. Next morning costume and make-up people came to the hotel, got me ready and took me to the set: a tourist tour boat on the canal, with twenty Extras. I performed as 'Hercule Poirot' all day, being a tour guide, standing at the front of the boat with a microphone, pointing out the places of interest to a bunch of my fellow SAs.
>
> The idea of the commercial was 'you do not have to be a well known detective to understand the new Denmark telephone directory' (don't ask me how that fits in with what I did!). After being a star for the day, I was shipped back to the UK on the Saturday night — job done. The commercial ended up being shown all over Denmark, and I got a very nice fee!
>
> **Ray Donn**

You should realise that some European countries do not have the infrastructure that the UK has to offer. In France, for example, a lot of films are made, but they tend to be low to mid-budget and large crowd scenes are rare. SA casting agencies don't really exist in France, and quite a few other countries. Most Assistant Directors in such places have their own personal book of people they like to use. They then lend each other their own books, or just cast people locally wherever they are shooting.

Having said that, other countries can have even cheaper production costs and be more attractive to Hollywood than the UK. Recently the Czech Republic was used as medieval England for *A Knight's Tale*, and Prague was the setting for Jack the Ripper's London in *From Hell*.

'Bollywood' in India and the rest of Asia are two of the biggest film-making territories in the world. Whilst their films are becoming more popular in the West, production is fairly insular and opportunities for SAs from outside these regions are rare (although quite a few Bollywood productions have come to film in the UK in recent years). Outside of Hollywood and the EU, the last five years have seen a growth for Australia and New Zealand, with Fox studios in Sydney being home to Hollywood films like *Star Wars: Attack of the Clones*, *The Matrix* and *Mission: Impossible II*. This has spurred a growth of Hollywood-backed homegrown talent in Australasia, particularly with Peter Jackson's *Lord of the Rings* trilogy in New Zealand and Baz Luhrmann's *Moulin Rouge*, also shot in Sydney.

## WORKING AS AN SA IN THE US

Working as an SA in the US is similar to the UK in some ways, but very different in others. It is similar in that one geographical area, Los Angeles (like London in the UK), has a higher concentration of film work than the rest of the country. Also like in the UK, most big cities have at least one casting agency that deals with SAs. Both New York and Chicago are major production centres. The US also has plenty of scam agencies taking large sums of money from unsuspecting potential artistes. Typically, you shouldn't pay more than $25 to $50 to register with a US casting agency.

In the US a production is either union or non-union. Within a union production, a contracted amount of SAs need to be SAG (Screen Actors Guild) members (contact details can be found at the back of this book). SAs used under SAG contracts are protected in a similar way to those with Equity and the FAA in the UK. On some productions, after a certain number of SAG-contracted SA positions have been filled, it is possible to work without being a SAG member. SAG says: "Typically, performers work in non-union background and principal roles in the early stages of their careers. Screen Actors Guild's interaction with performers begins after they have achieved professional status." Because union members receive a higher rate of pay than non-union artistes, it is quite normal for the non-union artistes to receive more work offers. Conversely, SAG members tend to be treated better and end up earning more money. The basic pay for SAG members to do background work on TV or a film is currently $100 for eight hours. The ninth and tenth hours are then paid at time-and-a-half, and after that it is double. Non-union SAs could be looking at as little as $40 per day.

Like Equity and the FAA, you have to pay to be a member of SAG. An interesting difference to the UK is that SAG represents actors as well as SAs; when doing background work in the US you are treated as a non-speaking actor. In a similar way to Equity, you also have to show evidence of at least three SAG contracts to become a member of SAG. The initial fee is fairly hefty, with an additional annual renewal fee of about $100 per year. You should be aware however that as a UK citizen, you can't just turn up in Hollywood and look for work as an SA without a work permit. You have to apply via the US embassy in London (address at the back of the book), but be warned, they are very tricky — if not impossible — to get.

## THE FUTURE FOR THE UK

Work opportunities for SAs are increasing in some areas and decreasing in others. In the UK these days it's a case of two steps forward and one step back, it seems. On the negative side, special effects are being used for big crowd scenes (and that's the case throughout the film industry, worldwide). A production that may once have used thousands of SAs for a sequence will now use a few hundred, and then replicate them using computers. A pessimistic view might suggest that one day all SAs will be computer generated. On the positive side though, the growth in digital television and the Internet is creating more opportunities for SAs in both commercials and TV drama.

So why is the UK still attractive to film-makers? As I pointed out at the beginning of this book, it's the reputation of its technicians and facilities as the best in the world — and the UK's Supporting Artistes are an essential part of that reputation. Despite its difficulties, the British film industry is still on fairly solid ground, and while economic conditions remain favourable, Hollywood will continue to find production costs in the UK considerably cheaper than filming in the US. Combined with a steady supply of home-produced films, demand for SAs is as high as it has ever been.

# THAT'S A WRAP!

I hope this book has achieved its aim of being a handy guide for both those wanting to start, and those already working as an SA. The key to enjoying background work is that it's *fun*. Film-making is a unique business, and being part of it should be rewarding. Though it can be a bit of a thankless task at times, if you approach SA work with energy and enthusiasm, you'll soon find yourself having a good time. Whichever way you approach it, if you are of the right mindset to enjoy the long hours and snatched glimpses of yourself on celluloid, then you shouldn't be disappointed with your experiences. If you are a new-comer to the world of Supporting Artistes, and this book has inspired you to try and get work, I wish you the best of luck. And if you have been doing the job for a while, here's to your continued success. Despite it being such a thankless task, you are a major part of the film-ing process. No one else will say it, so I will — thank you!

To round things off, here's a story that brilliantly sums up what life as an SA can be like if you're *really* lucky. Just think, this could be you...

I had one surreal week. For five days I was at Pinewood, as the Stand-in for the actor playing Colonel Moon in the twentieth James Bond film, *Die Another Day*. Helicopters exploded, fast cars were shot at, and hovercraft sprayed mud everywhere. You'll imagine my surprise when at one point between takes, Pierce Brosnan came up and asked me about the book I was reading: *How to Pass the Police Initial Recruitment Test*. I said I was hoping to join the Metropolitan Police. Brosnan replied that he'd already done that. He had got as far as being fitted for his uniform at the police training college in Hendon, having passed all the tests. "Why did you give it up then?"

I asked. "I got my first acting job!" he told me.

Unbelievably, just a couple of days later I found myself working on *Star Wars: Attack of the Clones*. I was transformed into the alien character Passel Argente as, basically, my double chin fitted best into his prosthetic one! It was the very last day of reshoots in Elstree and of course, I counted myself as incredibly fortunate to be there. It took two hours to have my new face pasted on and painted green before I was shown onto the set, an expanse of blue screen. I was to 'watch' a battle taking place on some distant desert as Count Dooku, played by Christopher Lee, says, "I did not realise the Jedi could muster such an army." That was pretty much what took place all day.

The really astonishing part though was when, at lunch, *George Lucas* came over and asked me about my book! We then talked about the differences between British and American police, I think — I'm afraid I don't remember much about it, as I was too busy screaming to myself, "Bugger me, first James Bond, now I'm having lunch with George Lucas!"

**Nick Field**

# APPENDICES

**SAMPLE SALARY VOUCHER/RELEASE FORM**

| | | | |
|---|---|---|---|
| | | NO: **71801** | |
| | | ARTISTES **SALARY VOUCHER** | |

**DATE WORKED:**

| | |
|---|---|
| Name | time arrived |
| Production Title | time produced |
| Production Company | time dismissed |

**THIS VOUCHER, DULY COMPLETED MUST BE PRESENTED FOR SIGNATURE BY THE ASSISTANT DIRECTOR WITHIN 30 MINUTES OF DISMISSAL**

| | | | | |
|---|---|---|---|---|
| Daily Rate | £ | Character | Make-Up Dept | |
| Holiday Pay | £ | | | |
| Overtime | £ | | time | |
| Early Call | £ | Category | Prop Dept | |
| Supp Service Fee | £ | Category | | |
| Supp. Performance | £ | Details | time | |
| Meal Allowance/s | £ | Details | Wardrobe Dept | |
| Travel Allowance/s | £ | Date | | |
| Fitting Fee / Audition | £ | | time | |
| Gross | £ | VAT No. | | |
| VAT @ % | £ | N.I. No. MUST COMPLETE: | | |
| Less N.I. | £ | NI EXEMPT [ ] | tick if exempt from NI | |
| NET Total | £ | Time Called: | Time Finished: | |

DEEMED IN FULL SETTLEMENT OF ALL SERVICES TO DATE

**SIGNED:**

FOR AND ON BEHALF OF THE PRODUCTION ( ASSISTANT DIRECTOR )

**SIGNED:**     **PRINT NAME:**

( THE ARTISTE )     I HAVE READ AND ACCEPT THE TERMS & CONDITIONS AS PRINTED OVERLEAF

**ADDRESS**     TEL NO

| | | |
|---|---|---|
| **WHITE COPY:** ASSOCIATE | **PINK COPY:** CASTING COLLECTIVE | **GREEN COPY:** ARTISTE |

# YOU CAN BE A MOVIE EXTRA

This will confirm my consent to your making motion picture and still photographs of me and/or sound recordings of my voice (and thereafter to dub my voice into any language) and/or instrumental and/or other sound effects in connection with the Film and that you, your affiliates, successors and assigns ("you") may distribute and exhibit all or any part thereof by and in any media (now known or hereafter created) throughout the world in perpetuity, without restriction, whether as part of the Film or otherwise. This consent shall also extend to include, inter alia, any advertising, publicity, merchandise, commodities, by-products and tie-ins in connection with the Film. I acknowledge that you shall be the owner of such motion picture and still photographs and sound recordings, and nothing herein contained shall obligate you to include same in the Film, or otherwise.

I hereby grant and assign all rights and consents to you (including rental and lending rights) under the Copyright, Designs and Patents Act 1988, or any statutory modification thereof, or under similar legislation in other countries of the world and irrevocably and unconditionally waive the benefit of any provision of law known as "moral rights" or "droit moral" now or hereafter existing.

I hereby undertake that I will not at any time issue or authorise publicity or disclose any confidential information relating to this engagement or any persons engaged in connection with the Film (as distinguished from personal publicity relating solely to me) to the press or media without your prior written consent in each case.

I hereby acknowledge that I have recieved good and valuable consideration in respect of the consents and rights granted hereunder and I further acknowledge that such consideration is in full and final settlement thereof. I further acknowledge that such consideration includes equitable remuneration for the rental and lending right assigned herein.

This release shall be binding upon, and shall inure to the benefit of, my heirs, executors, administrators, successors and assigns.

I confirm that I am a British citizen ordinarily resident in the UK or a citizen ordinarily resident in another country which is a member of the European Union or the Commonwealth.

# APPENDICES

## SAMPLE AGENCY CONTRACT

Here's an example of the kind of contract your agency will ask you to sign when you join their books. This sample uses the fictitious company 'The Sample Agency'. The contract you sign may not be identical to this one, but it should be similar.

**1)** 'The Sample Agency' will act as your agent and try to find you work as a background artiste with production companies. 'The Sample Agency' will charge you 15% commission (plus VAT) of each interim payment received for each placement found for you and will deduct the commission from payment received from the production company on your behalf. Where you have received payment directly from the production company 'The Sample Agency' will invoice you for any commission owing, which will be a VAT invoice, where appropriate.

**2)** Whilst working as a background artiste your employment status will be dependent upon the specific contract with the production company. Nothing in this agreement shall render you an employee of 'The Sample Agency' in any way.

**3)** Payment from the production company will be received by 'The Sample Agency' on your behalf. Payment will be deposited into a client account. Once payment has been received by 'The Sample Agency' on your behalf (this is normally four to six weeks after you have completed the work assigned) 'The Sample Agency' will after making a deduction of 15% commission (plus VAT) as set out in clause 1 above, pay the balance of the payment directly into your bank account by BACS within 10 days. A remittance will be posted to you at the address you have given to us.

**4)** It is your responsibility to make sure that the bank details and address we have for you are correct, and to inform 'The Sample Agency' of any changes as and when they occur. 'The Sample Agency' will not process this data in any way that is incompatible with the Data Protection Act.

**5)** 'The Sample Agency' cannot pass payment from a production company on to you until payment has been made by the production company. You will normally receive payment four to six weeks after the day that you worked.

**6)** As your agent, it is our responsibility to deal with any problems that may arise when you are on set. Therefore in this instance it is your responsibility to contact 'The Sample Agency' and not the production company.

**7)** It is your responsibility to get to any location at the call time you are given. It is your responsibility to phone 'The Sample Agency' the day before you work to be given locations and call time details; this is always between 5pm and 6pm. We reserve the right to replace you if you do not call in at the allotted time.

**8)** On Film and TV sets you will be given a salary voucher at the beginning of each filming day. It is your responsibility to keep hold of this and to make sure it is signed at the end of each day by the Assistant Director. The production company may refuse to make payment where this has not been complied with. Where payment is not made by the production company through your negligence or carelessness 'The Sample Agency' reserves the right to charge you a fee of 15% of the value of work.

**9)** On commercials, photographic stills, pop promos and corporate videos you might not receive a salary voucher. It is your responsibility to keep a record of times and dates that you worked.

**10)** 'The Sample Agency' is not liable for any loss of or damage to any of your personal possessions or personal injury when you are on set.

**11)** You are not allowed to take any photographs on any set, or contact any journalist or publication regarding the work you have done on any production.

**12)** We cannot guarantee you work on any production. We are not obliged to contact you with any work opportunities with production companies. You are not obliged to accept any work offered to you.

**13)** You are required to comply with any rules and regulations set by the production company. We reserve the right to refuse to give you work, if your behaviour is deemed by 'The Sample Agency' or the production company as unacceptable or inappropriate, or if you misrepresent 'The Sample Agency' in any way, or if your behaviour is deemed unacceptable towards a member of 'The Sample Agency' or any production staff member.

This is a contract only with 'The Sample Agency' and not with any production company. You may be required to enter into a separate contract with the production company, which will be between you and the production company only.

By signing this document you are agreeing to the above terms and conditions of 'The Sample Agency'.

I_____have read the contract and accept the above terms and conditions

Signed _____
Dated _____

---

## SUPPORTING ARTISTES' AGENCIES

Agencies come and go all the time. The ones listed below were at least all fairly well established at the time of writing. However, always make sure you are satisfied of an agency's trustworthiness before parting with any money.

**London and the South-East**

Broadcasting
Unit 23
Canalot Studios
222 Kensal Road
London, W10 5BN
Tel: 020 7460 5222
Fax: 020 7460 5223

Casting Collective Ltd, The
Olympic House
317-321 Latimer Road
London, W10 6RA
Tel: 020 8962 0099
Fax: 020 8962 0003
enquiries@castingcollective.co.uk
www.castingcollective.co.uk

Casting Network
Tel: 020 8339 9090
Fax: 020 8390 0605
www.thecastingnetwork.co.uk

David Agency, The
153 Battersea Rise
London, SW11 1HP
Tel: 020 7223
Fax: 020 7924 2334
www.davidagency.net

Elliott Agency
PO Box 2772
Lewes
East Sussex, BN8 4DW
Tel: 01273 401 264
Fax: 01273 400 814

Extras Unlimited
14 Russell Garden Mews
London, W14 8EU
Tel: 020 7603 9995
Fax: 020 7602 9994
www.extrasunlimited.com

FBI
4th Floor
20-24 Kirby Street
London, EC1N 8TS
Tel: 020 7242 5542
Fax: 020 7242 8125
www.fullybooked-inc.com

Fresh Agents
Albert House
82 Queens Road
Brighton
East Sussex, BN1 3XE
Tel: 01273 711 777
Fax: 01273 711 778
www.freshagents.com

G2
15 Lexham Mews
London, W8 6JW
Tel: 020 7376 2133
Fax: 020 7376 2416

Jaclyn Agency
Thackeray House
Hempnall
Norwich, NR15 2LP
Tel: 01508 499 241
Fax: 01508 499 241

Jayne Collins
38 Commercial Street
London, E1 6LP
Tel: 020 7422 0014
Fax: 020 7422 0015
www.jaynecollinscasting.com

JB Agency
7 Stonehill Mansions
8 Streatham High Road
London, SW16 1DD
Tel: 020 8677 7202
Fax: 020 8769 9567
www.jb-agency.com

Lee's People
60 Poland Street
London, W1V 3DF
Tel: 020 7734 5775
Fax: 020 7734 3033
www.lees-people.com

Mad Dog
56 Camden High Street
Camden
London, NW1 0NE
Tel: 020 7916 1511
Fax: 020 7916 1511
www.mad-dog-casting.co.uk

Ray Knight
12a Lambolle Place
London, NW3 4PG
Tel: 020 7722 4111
Fax: 020 7722 2322
www.rayknightcasting.co.uk

Screenlite
Studio 61
Shepperton Studios
Studios Road
Shepperton
Middlesex, TW17 0QD
Tel: 01932 562 611
Fax: 01932 572 507

Solomon Artistes
30 Clarence Street
Southend-on-Sea
Essex, SS1 1BD
Tel: 01702 392 370
Fax: 01702 392 385
www.solomon-artistes.co.uk

2020
2020 Hopgood Street
London, W12 7JU
Tel: 020 8746 2020
Fax: 020 8735 2727
www.2020casting.com

**The South West**

Phoenix
1a Cornwallis Crescent
Clifton
Bristol, BS8 4PL
Tel: 0117 973 1100
Fax: 0117 973 4160

South West Casting
The Courtyard
Whitchurch
Ross on Wye
Herefordshire, HR9 6DA
Tel: 01600 892 005
Fax: 01600 891 099
www.southwestcasting.co.uk

**The Midlands and the North**

ATS Casting
26 St Michaels Road
Headingley
Yorkshire, LS6 3AW
Tel: 0113 230 4300
Fax: 0113 230 4300

Celex Casting
11 Glencroft Drive
Stenson Fields
Derby, DE24 3LS
Tel: 01332 232 445
Fax: 01332 232 115

Intercity Casting
Portland Tower
Portland Street
Manchester, M1 3LF
Tel: 0161 226 0103
Fax: 0161 226 0103
www.iccast.co.uk

Janet Howe Agency
Studio 1
Whitebridge Estates
Whitebridge Lane
Stone
Staffordshire, ST15 8LQ
Tel: 01785 816 888
Fax: 01785 816 888

Lakeside Casting
63 Scotland Road
Carlisle
Cumbria, CA3 9HT
Tel: 01228 401 093
Fax: 01228 401 093

Northern Professionals
21 Cresswell Avenue

North Shields
Tyne and Wear, NE29 9BQ
Tel: 0191 257 8635
Fax: 0191 296 3243

PHA Casting
Tanzaro House
Ardwick Green North
Manchester
Lancashire, M12 6FZ
Tel: 01612 734 444
Fax: 01612 734 567
www.pha-agency.co.uk

Pride Management
The Burnside Centre
38 Burnside Crescent
Middleton
Manchester
Lancashire, M24 5NN
Tel: 01616 436 266
Fax: 01616 436 266

Special Acting Services
23 New Mount Street
Manchester
Lancashire, M4 4DE
Tel: 0161 953 4103
Fax: 0161 953 4103

**Scotland**

Cairns Agency
Ladywell House
94 Duke Street
Glasgow, G4 0UW
Tel: 0141 763 1435
Fax: 0141 778 0403

Extra Special Casting
Greyfriars Riding School
Blantyre Farm Road
Uddingston, G71 7RN
Tel: 0141 641 2843
Fax: 0141 641 2843

Liz Bisset Management
Heronbrook
Ladeside
Newmilns
Ayrshire, KA16 9BE

Tel: 01560 320 782
Fax: 01560 322 952

United Casting
Craighall House
58A High Craighall Road
Glasgow, G4 9UD
Tel: 0141 333 9890
Fax: 0141 333 1771
www.unitedcasting.co.uk

**Wales**

Cardiff Casting
Chapter Arts Centre
Market Road
Cardiff , CF5 1QE
Tel: 029 2023 3321
Fax: 029 2023 3380
www.ukactors.co.uk

Edward Wyman Agency
67 Llanon Road
Llanishen
Cardiff, CF14 5AH
Tel: 029 2075 2351
Fax: 029 2075 2444
www.wymancasting.fsnet.co.uk

Oska's
PO Box 362
Castle Street
Cardiff, CF10 1YQ
Tel: 029 2031 1500
Fax: 029 2031 1500
www.oskas.com

# SPECIALIST AGENCIES

**Child Agencies**

Allsorts Agency
45 Victoria Road
South Woodford
London, E18 1JL
Tel: 020 8491 7000
Fax: 020 8491 7001
www.allsorts-agency.com

Barbara Speake Stage School
East Acton Lane

London, W3 7EG
Tel: 020 8743 6096
Fax: 020 8933 3418

Boden Agency
6 Windmill Hill
Enfield
Middlesex, EN2 6SA
Tel: 020 8367 2692
Fax: 020 8367 1836
www.bodenstudios.com

Bubblegum
Ardreigh
Beaconsfield Road
Farnham
Bucks, SL2 3BP
Tel: 01753 646 348
Fax: 0870 051 6779

Children of London Agency
273 Malden Rd
New Malden
Surrey, KT3 6AH
Tel: 020 8949 0450
Fax: 020 8949 0522

Italia Conti Academy of Theatre Arts
Italia Conti House
23 Goswell Road
London, EC1M 7AJ
Tel: 020 7608 0047
Fax: 020 7253 1430

Kids Plus Agency
54 Grove Park
London, SE5 8LG
Tel: 020 7737 3901
Fax: 020 7737 3901

Lamont Casting
94 Harington Road
Formby
Liverpool, L37 1PZ
Tel: 01704 877 024
Fax: 01704 872 422

Little Acorns Model Agency
London House
271-273 King Street
Hammersmith

London, W6 9LZ
Tel: 020 8563 0773
Fax: 020 8408 3077
www.littleacorns.co.uk

Norrie Carr Agency & Drama School
Holborn Studios
49 Eagle Wharf Road
London, N1 7ED
Tel: 020 7253 1771
Fax: 020 7253 1772
www.norriecarr.com

Ravenscourt Management
Tandy House
30-40 Dalling Road
London, W6 OJB
Tel: 020 8741 0707
Fax: 020 8741 1786

Redroofs Theatre School
Littlewick Green
Maidenhead
Berkshire, SL6 3QY
Tel: 01628 822 982
Fax: 01628 822 461
www.redroofs.co.uk

Whizz Kids Stage & Screen Company
3 Marshall Road
Cambridge, CB1 7TY
Tel: 01223 512 423
Fax: 01223 512 423
www.whizzkidsdrama.co.uk

Young'uns Agency
Sylvia Young Theatre School
6 Rossmore Road,
London, NW1 6NJ
Tel: 020 7723 0037
Fax: 020 7723 1040

## Ethnic Agencies

Ethnic Artistes
118a Tonsley Heights
East Hill
Wandsworth
London, SW18 2HF
Tel: 020 8877 9324
Fax: 020 8874 3382

Oriental Casting
No 1 Wyatt Park Road
Streatham Hill
London, SW2 3TN
Tel: 020 8671 8538
Fax: 020 8674 9303
www.orientalcasting.com

## Hand-modelling Agency

Derek's Hands
153 Battersea Rise
London, SW11 1HP
Tel: 020 7924 2484
Fax: 020 7924 2334
www.derekshands.com

## Look-alike Agency

Susan Scott Lookalikes
Tel: 020 7387 9245
Fax: 020 7722 8261
www.lookalikes-susanscott.co.uk

## Police Agencies

Cops on the Box
Tel: 020 8679 3611
Fax: 020 8679 5661

PACE
Suite 501
International House
Regent Street
London, W1R 8QD
Tel: 01753 674 112
Fax: 01753 673 272
pace999.hypermart.net

## Short Actor Agency

Willow Management
151 Main Street
Yaxley
Peterborough
Cambs, PE7 3LD
Tel: 01733 240 392
Fax: 01733 240 392
www.willowmanagement.co.uk

## Sports Agencies

Acrobat Productions
The Circus Space
Coronet Street
London, N1 6HD
Tel: 020 7613 5259
Fax: 020 7613 5259
www.acrobatproductions.co.uk

Circus Maniacs
Office 8A
The Kingswood Foundation
Britannia Road
Kingswood
Bristol, BS15 8DB
Tel: 0117 947 7042
Fax: 0117 947 7042
www.circusmaniacs.com

Physicality
265-267 Ilford Lane
Essex, IG1 ZSD
Tel: 020 8491 2800
Fax: 020 8491 2801
www.physicality.co.uk

Twist & Flic
1A Calton Avenue
Dulwich Village
London, SE21 7DE
Tel: 020 8299 8800
Fax: 020 8299 8600
www.sportsmodels.com

## Twins Agencies

PC Theatrical Twins & Triplets
10 Strathmore Gardens
Edgeware
Middlesex, HA8 5HJ
Tel: 020 8381 2229
Fax: 020 8933 3418
www.twinagency.com

Twins & Triplets
Holmhurst Road
Upper Belvedere, DA17 6HW
Tel: 01322 440 184
Fax: 01322 440 184
www.twins.triplets.freeuk.com

## Ugly Agency

Ugly
Tigris House
256 Edgware Road
London, W2 1DS
Tel: 020 7402 5564
Fax: 020 7402 0507
www.ugly.org

## Voiceover Agencies

Another Tongue Voices
48 Dean Street
London, W1V 5HL
Tel: 020 7494 0300
www.anothertongue.com

Hobson's Voices
62 Chiswick High Road
London, W4 1SY
Tel: 020 8995 3628
Fax: 020 8742 1511
www.hobsons-international.com

Talkies Ltd
3 Charlotte Mews
London, W1T 4DZ
Tel: 020 7323 6883
www.talkies.ltd.uk

# STUDIOS

BBC Elstree Studios
Clarendon Road
Borehamwood, WD6 1JF
Tel: 020 8953 6100

BBC Television Centre
Wood Lane
London, W12 7TS
Tel: 020 8743 8000
Fax: 020 8743 8000

Black Island Studios
9-11 Alliance Road
Acton
London, W3 0RA
Tel: 020 8752 1700
Fax: 020 8752 1112
www.blackislandstudios.co.uk

Bray Studios
Down Place
Water Oakley
Windsor Road
Windsor
Berkshire, SL4 5UG
Tel: 020 8567 6655
Fax: 020 8758 8658

Carlton Studios
Lenton Lane
Nottingham, NG7 2NA
Tel: 0115 964 5320
Fax: 0115 964 5755

Cheltenham Studios
Arle Court
Hatherley Lane
Cheltenham
Gloucestershire, GL51 6PN
Tel: 01242 542700
Fax: 01242 542701
www.cheltstudio.com

Dukes Island Studios
2 Dukes Road
Acton
London, W3 0SL
Tel: 020 8956 5600
Fax: 020 8956 5604

Ealing Studios
Ealing Green
Ealing
London, W5 5EP
Tel: 020 8567 6655
Fax: 020 8758 8658
www.ealingstudios.com

Elstree Film Studios
Shenley Road
Borehamwood
Hertfordshire, WD6 1JG
Tel: 020 8953 6100
Fax: 020 8905 1135

Granada (Manchester)
Quay Street
Manchester, M60 9EA
Tel: 0161 827 2275
Fax: 0161 832 8809

Greenford Studios
5-11 Taunton Road
Metropolitan Centre
Greenford
Middlesex, UB6 8QU
Tel: 020 8575 7300
Fax: 020 8578 1536

HDS Redditch
2e Eagle Road
North Moons Moat Industrial Estate
Redditch
Birmingham, B98 9HD
Tel: 0152 76 2822
Fax: 0152 76 8436

Leavesden Studios
South Way
Leavesden
Watford
Hertfordshire, WD2 7LT
Tel: 01923 685 060
Fax: 01923 685 061

Pinewood Studios
Pinewood Road
Iver
Bucks, SL0 0NH
Tel: 01753 651 700
Fax: 01753 656 844
www.pinewood-studios.co.uk

Riverside Studios
Crisp Road
London, W6 9RL
Tel: 020 8237 1000
Fax: 020 8237 1011
www.riversidestudios.co.uk

Shepperton Studios
Studios Road
Shepperton
Middlesex, TW17 0QJ
Tel: 01932 562 611
Fax: 01932 568 989
www.sheppertonstudios.com

Teddington Studios
Broom Road
Teddington
Middlesex, TW11 9NT

Tel: 020 8977 3253
Fax: 020 8943 4050
www.teddington.co.uk

Three Mills Studios
Three Mills Lane
London, E3 3DU
Tel: 020 7363 0033
Fax: 020 7363 0034
www.threemills.com

Twickenham Studios
The Barons
St Margarets
Twickenham
Middlesex, TW1 2AW
Tel: 020 8607 8888
Fax: 020 8607 8889
www.twickenhamstudios.com

Westway Studios
8 Olaf Street
London, W11 4BE
Tel: 020 7221 9041
Fax: 020 7221 9399

Yorkshire Television
The Television Centre
Leeds, LS3 1JS
Tel: 0113 222 7807
Fax: 0113 245 4319

## COSTUME FITTERS

Angels & Burmans
1 Garrick Road
London, NW9 6AA
Tel: 020 8202 2244
Fax: 020 8202 1820
www.angels.uk.com

Carlo Manzi Rentals
31-33 Liddell Road
Maygrove Road
London, NW6 2EW
Tel: 020 7625 6391
Fax: 020 7625 5386

Cosprops
26-28 Rochester Place
London, NW1 9JR

Tel: 020 7485 6731
Fax: 020 7485 5942
www.cosprop.co.uk

## UNION AND OTHER USEFUL ADDRESSES

BECTU (FAA)
373-377 Clapham Road
London, SW9 9BT
Tel: 020 7346 0900,
info@bectu.org.uk
www.bectu.org.uk

British Film Commission
10 Little Portland Street
London, W1W 7JG
Tel: 020 7861 7860
Fax: 020 7861 7864
www.bfc.co.uk

Department of Trade
and Industry (DTI)
UG65
1 Victoria Street
London, SW1H 0ET
Tel: 020 7215 5000
Fax: 020 7215 5788
www.dti.gov.uk

Equity
Guild House
Upper St Martin's Lane
London, WC2H 9EG
Tel: 020 7379 6000
info@equity.org.uk
www.equity.org.uk

Musicians Union
60/62 Clapham Road
London, SW9 0JJ
Tel: 020 7582 5566
Fax: 020 7582 9805
info@musiciansunion.org.uk
www.musiciansunion.org.uk

Screen Actors Guild (SAG)
5757 Wilshire Blvd
Los Angeles
CA 90036, USA
Tel: (001 323) 954 1600

# YOU CAN BE A MOVIE EXTRA

Fax: (001 323) 549 6603
www.sag.com

Stage Newspaper, The
Stage House
47 Bermondsey Street
London, SE1 3XT
Tel: 020 7403 1818
Fax: 020 7357 9287
www.thestage.co.uk

United States Embassy
24 Grosvenor Square
London, W1A 1AE
www.usembassy.org.uk

## USEFUL INTERNET SITES

### Planning Your Journey by Car

AA route planner
www.theaa.com

Maporama
www.maporama.com

Multimap
www.multimap.co.uk

NCP car parks
www.ncp.co.uk

Streetmap
www.streetmap.co.uk

### Planning Your Journey by Public Transport

London Transport
Tel: 020 7222 1234
www.londontransport.com

National rail enquiries
Tel: 08457 48 49 50
www.nationalrail.co.uk

Train times
www.thetrainline.com

The Tube
www.thetube.com

### Advice From Other Artistes' Internet Sites

Casting Collective Forum
www.castingcollective.co.uk/forums
Advice from a collective group of
Supporting Artistes.

The Hidden Extra
www.hiddenextra.com
Advice offered by anonymous working
Supporting Artistes.

### Upcoming Film News/Rumours

Ain't It Cool News
www.aintitcool.com

CHUD (Cinematic Happenings Under
Development)
www.chud.com

Dark Horizons
www.darkhorizons.com

Empire Online
www.empireonline.co.uk

Internet Movie Database, The
www.imdb.co.uk

Up Coming Movies
www.upcomingmovies.com

## A-Z OF TERMINOLOGY

(See also 'Who's Who'? and 'Terms You Will Hear On Set' in Chapter 4.)

**Backlot:** Americanism, an open-air part of the studio, where sets are built.

**Blonde:** Type of light.

**Bluescreen:** Sometimes called greenscreen or chroma-key. Filming takes place against a blue or green background. The background can then be replaced by a different location.

**Body Cast:** Occasionally you may be asked to go to a body cast. A cast will be made of part of your body, or even your whole body.

**Bookers:** Sometimes called Casting Co-ordinators. The people who ring you from the agency to book you for work. These are the people you need to be friends with most.

**Boom:** The pole that the Boom Operator holds, attached to an overhead microphone.

**Broken Lunch:** An additional payment made if you are not given a meal break within a set time. Usually only paid on film sets.

**Call In:** Normal procedure is to call your agent the night before you work to find out your call time and location

**Call Sheet:** A daily report normally produced by the 2nd AD, given out to the crew so they know what is being filmed that day.

**Call Time:** This is the time you must report to your given location. You *must* be on time.

**Camera Right and Camera Left:** These terms describe the view from the camera's point of view. So if you are told to move camera left and you are facing the camera, you would actually move to your right, and vice versa.

**Chit/Voucher:** This is your paperwork, given to you when you arrive on set. You must get it signed before you leave, to ensure you get paid.

**Clapperboard:** Sometimes called the slate. It is used to mark each take by number and helps the Editor synchronise sound and vision.

**Close-up Shot:** Of a person, the camera would be only filming their head.

**Confirmed Booking:** This is a firm commitment to work on this day. Do not take another job.

**Continuity:** A sequence filming over more than one day, or more than one shot. It is therefore essential that nothing changes and upsets the continuity of the scene.

**Continuous Working Day:** A filming day where you will not be given a meal break, but a running buffet is provided while filming continues.

**Costume Fitting:** You will sometimes be required to have a costume fitted before the filming day. You may also be asked to go to a wig fitting or a prosthetics fitting.

**Crane Shot:** The camera may pan up at great height. A crane is used to lift the camera into the air.

**Crowd Base:** On bigger calls this is where you will be asked to report.

**Dolly:** Equipment that carries the camera during tracking shots.

**Double:** A person used when the actor is not needed, or available. Usually shot from long distance or from behind, or just a part of the body, such as hands.

**Establisher Shot:** A general view of any location or building.

**Eye Line:** The direction you are required to look in during a take.

**Gel:** Something that covers a light to create different effects.

**Honey Wagon:** The toilet.

**Insert:** Close-ups of particular importance, for example a hand picking up a gun.

**Long Shot:** Covers the whole height of a person, with some of the background.

**Look-alike Double:** An artiste who is used because they have a strong physical resemblance to an actor.

**Master Shot:** Covers the main action all the way through with a wide shot.

**Mid Shot:** Of a person, the camera would be on the top half of their body.

# YOU CAN BE A MOVIE EXTRA

**Multi-episodic:** An additional payment paid under some agreements if more than one episode of a production is recorded in one day.

**Nepotism:** Something you have to get used to in the film business.

**Pan:** The camera moves from left to right, or right to left.

**Pencilled Booking:** A provisional booking, yet to be confirmed. Sometimes you may be given a 'heavy pencil', this is more likely to happen, but still not confirmed.

**Pick-up:** A small part of a scene that has been missed, or needs to be reshot.

**Prop:** Any object you may be given, in addition to your costume, that is movable, such as a sword or rifle.

**Prosthetic:** An artificial body part, applied in the make-up department.

**Redhead:** Another type of light.

**Reverse Shot:** A 180-degree angle from the last position of the camera.

**Rushes:** A first look at what has been filmed on a given day.

**Shift Call:** Only used under the FAA agreement. Not a full day, it is a maximum of four hours' work.

**Soundstage:** At the studios, an enclosed space where the set is constructed.

**Spark:** Another name for an electrician.

**Special Effects:** Can be anything used in shot, such as fire, wind, rain or snow.

**Speed:** The camera has reached its required speed.

**Squib:** An explosive charge used to create the effect of a bullet or small explosion.

**Stand-in:** A person used in place of an actor to set up initial lighting and camera. Usually of a similar height, age and skin tone to the actor.

**Take:** Filming of a particular sequence. This will be repeated until the director is happy.

**Tilt:** The camera moves either up or down.

**Tracking Shot or Dolly:** The camera moves smoothly forwards or backwards by running on tracks.

**Unit Base:** Where the production team will base itself on any given day when on location.

**Walk-on:** Someone the viewer may identify as an individual, who may have a few words to say. A step up from background work.

**Wild Track:** A recording of atmospheric sound.

**Wrap:** This indicates the end of the filming day.

## ABOUT THE AUTHOR

Rob Martin is one of four founding Directors of The Casting Collective Ltd, which was formed in 1999. Before that he worked with the same three colleagues at another casting agency in London.

## ABOUT THE CASTING COLLECTIVE

The team now at The Casting Collective has been responsible for casting SAs and Walk-ons for many of the big films and TV dramas filmed in the UK over the last five years. Some of the bigger productions the team has worked on since forming The Casting Collective include *About a Boy* (2002), *Band of Brothers* (2001), *Gosford Park* (2001), *Harry Potter and the Chamber of Secrets* (2002), *Harry Potter and the Philosopher's Stone* (2001), *Lara Croft: Tomb Raider* (2001), *Spy Game* (2001) and *Star Wars: Episode II — Attack of the Clones* (2002, UK shoot). Productions the team worked on before they set up The Casting Collective include *East Is East* (1999), *Eyes Wide Shut* (1999), *The Fifth Element* (1997), *Gladiator* (2000), *The Mummy* (1999), *Notting Hill* (1999) and *Star Wars: Episode I — The Phantom Menace* (1999).